Episodes Intertwined

Episodes Intertwined

Collection of Poetry

3

1991–1999

Rosa M. Diaz

BOOKSIDE Press

BOOKSIDE Press

BookSide Press
877-741-8091
www.booksidepress.com
orders@booksidepress.com

For all single mothers

INTRODUCTION

This is the continuation to BETWEEN THE BOOKS, Collection of Poetry 2, 1983-1990.

With my graduation from the university, CSU Stanislaus, in 1990, a new phase of my life began. My son was born soon after I graduated and I went back home as a single mother. I was alone, jobless, destitute, unprepared for motherhood and depressed. However, I still managed to make the best with nothing at hand. My personal life was at its lowest point but, at the same time, I was at my highest point with the birth of my son. I was a proud momma and he brought me joys, hope, a new and positive perspective of life. I had someone to fight for and to live for.

I needed time to adjust to the new environment and it's ways but I forgot about me and only focused on my son's needs. My son had the love and attention from my family members but I felt he needed the father and his family too so I took my son to meet his other side of the family hoping they would love him and shower him with attention. It hurt and saddened me when this wasn't happening. They were hesitant to be part of his life and accept part of the responsibility that the father didn't want. It seemed they were always entangled in some sort of crucial problem that took their attention away. They were always leaving the child for a later time. It took me a very long time to accept that I did not see the love, the connection, the interest or the effort from their part to keep the relationship with the child so I stopped taking him to them. I tried. I feel I really tried but I felt I was begging them to love my child. I understood that they never liked me so, perhaps, for that reason, they were not loving my son either.

Looking back, I was greatly hurt that they were not giving my son all the attention and love because I still loved the man and it was hard to accept that we were no longer together. Little did I know that big problems and many factors were aligning against me. My ex sued me for full custody of my son and we were in and out of court for five years. After five years of fighting and tens of thousands of dollars wasted, I proved my innocence at the same time I was protecting my son away from vengeful people. I won.

Although I faced the world with a big bright smile, the long and deep sadness I went through during my pregnancy, still lingered after the birth and even several years later. I didn't realize the gravity of it but in those quiet moments alone, I saw how lonely I felt. I didn't understand it at the moment, but depression made me feel dissatisfied, unwanted and unloved. I felt a big void in my mind and felt lonely and alone against the world.

Yes, a child fulfills part of the void or need but it's not enough. Having a mate to love and who loves you and supports you, fulfills the other half of the void. I longed to have a special friend to talk to about anything. I needed someone to whisper the sweet nothings to my ear. I needed someone to flatter me once in a while. I needed a man to tell me how beautiful I looked. At the moment, I needed a man to make me feel important and worthy.

How wrong I was. I learned that the strength, pride, importance and value we think we need and deserve from others, comes from within ourselves and not by whom we have by our side. The void we may feel, is not really filled by the mate or the children we may have. The void is filled and covered by being at peace with ourselves, how positive we feel and how we see life. We need to accept all the mistakes we have made and know that we are not the only ones suffering this pain. And whatever is happening to us is not original or particular. Happiness is momentary and cheerfulness comes from within from the contentment in life.

I thought I needed a mate but I have never been the type to be out there on the lookout. So I stayed home. I closed the door and let time pass by, perhaps my prince charming would come and meet me at my doorstep. The man who appeared at my doorstep was no prince charming, that's for sure. He was a two-face monster, who was kind and charming and then secretly abusive. He was a typical male chauvinist. The first month was good. The second month, the control and manipulation began. The third month, when I ended the relationship, he became a danger with constant threats, blackmail, and accusations. But his intent to keep me under his control didn't work.

This was the second time I faced the monstrosity of the machismo. The first time, I was young, in love, inexperienced and blind. But now

I was able to see the signs and I set my boundaries. I defended myself and ended the relationship before it was too late.

I was fighting the same war with two men, like a two-headed monster that is the toxicity of the male superiority. One decided to fight me with a vengeance and made the excuse it was for the child. The other one was fighting me with the excuse of loving so much and I not letting him protect me. It took me a while to stop feeling sorry for myself but I got up and learned to fight. I got rid of both monsters because no one is going to dominate me with restrictions, screams and, much less, strikes.

I connected the internet service in my house in 1992. With the internet, as a social and information instrument, I picked up the qualities and good points from the people I met online. I met so many wonderful people online and offline who inspired me with their stories and advice to my personal problems. My perceptions on issues and my visual capacity expanded and changed. My opinions, my views, my self-worth also changed.

Even though I did not have that special mate, the emotional loneliness subsided as I connected with different people through a computer screen and in real life. Marriage was no longer the ultimate goal. With time, I came to accept that it was fine with me if I never found that special someone. I was well aware when, regarding marriage, I said, 'No, thank you. I had enough. I rather be on my own than be constantly dealing with a chauvinist man for the rest of my life.'

In the Content page, I wrote an S for the poems that were originally in Spanish and an E for the poems written in English.

CONTENTS

HEAVENLY

To cry or to pray,
I look down,
To defend, protect,
And advocate,
I look head on,
To implore
For health, peace,
Strength or life,
I look up to the heavens
With my arms extended
And open hands
So the heavens know
Where the pleading
And the prayers come from.

Angels From Heaven

Disguised by the skin,
The angels from up above
Couldn't spread out
Their wings on earth
And flew high into the sky
Until heaven was reached.

They came down
And borrowed
Time and space
To venture, learn,
Create and teach.

Angels from heaven
Take many forms
So we're never alone.
They're invisible
And, yet,
Share their warmth.

For our protection,
The angels from heaven
Form a barrier,
For our rescue
They form a bridge,
In so many forms,
They cover us
With their wings.

Then the Lord
Calls upon them,
They are captured
And we question
The meaning of life
That is held in a moment,
In a smile, in a tear,
In a dream, in a memory
Untouched, unseen.

When the angels
From heaven above
Don't have time
To say goodbye,
It hurts us forever
And we're left
With a full mind,
An empty spirit,
And a confused heart.
And, again, we wonder,
What do we need to quest
To fulfill our lives?

November 10, 1995

Fly

Fly high
Into the sky,
Fly away far,
Fly away strong,
Fly away alone,
Fly away brave.
Fly like a bird,
Fly like a plane.

Fly into the heavens,
Fly into the wind,
Fly above the clouds,
Fly all the way into the stars
For they know who you are.

As you come down,
Lower your guard
Free your thoughts,
And clean your spirit
From any emotional disease.
No matter if it's only in a dream,
Don't hesitate to cry,
To laugh or speak,
Find your truth
And make peace within
So even the dilemmas
Allow you to succeed.

August 10, 1997

Afloat

I fight against
Monsters, ogres,
Dragons, vampires
And snakes
In my nightmares
And in real life.
I fight to defend the child
From the claws of the beast
That frightens, destroys,
Spits, absorbs and constricts.

My reputation
Is on the grounds
Based on accusations,
Lies and exaggerations
That question my words,
My motives and my actions
As if he was pure,
Loyal and true.

The man didn't want the child,
His child,
But now fights for him
Out of revenge
And for a few dollars
That might be saved
And in the grownup battles,
The child becomes
The puppet to hurt the other.

Excuses come and go
Not to see the child
And blames everyone
But himself
As real man and true father
Will do everything
To see the child
And be part of his life.

But the man is my enemy
And with his soft voice,
Quick tongue
And convincing smile,
Is about to win custody.
Seems they listen
And feel for him,
Seems that in their eyes,
I am unfit.

Seems like he's taking
What I love the most,
My testimony doesn't matter,
Nobody listens,
Nobody helps,
Nobody pays attention,
Everyone is leaving
The child in the middle
Of the punishment.

I fight everyday
And don't know
How to turn this around,
One more word, one misstep,
He takes the prize
And I am on the brink
Of collapse.

I want to be strong and smart,
I need to prove
The kind of man
I am dealing with,
I need to prove
I am worthy of my son
To those who only see
The external side of me.

I am tired of living
On the defensive,
I wake up and fall asleep
Praying God
Gives me a new strategy
Where I am the accuser,
The attacker
And go on the offensive.

I made my prayers
Less wordy
And more direct.
I asked for the truth
To come afloat
So everyone can see
Who's honest
And who's the criminal.

Finally,
God heard my requests
And paved the way for me.
Enough with the mercy
For the man I once loved.
My hand gave the attack
Direct and definitive
And two quickly fell
Frightened

As if they were ambushed
Although they never were.
It was only truth
And persistence for justice
That never yielded.

In the sea of lies,
Truth came afloat,
My face came afloat
And I was able to breathe,
My child came afloat
And was able to live.
With one life jacket
We were able to escape.
The undignified people
Had their punishment
And those who didn't help
Also got what they deserved.

December 15, 1999

It's Sad

It's sad
To see someone go
But we have to say goodbye
And carry on.

Be strong, be brave.
Never lose
The power of faith.
Never lose sight
Of what's important in life.

I think of you
Frequently
And pray to God
For you.
I wish you the best
So you can come through
This one and all.

June 7, 1996

Behold,
The child is born,
The wait is over,
Thank the Lord.

The most beautiful thing
Descended from above,
He's precious,
Perfect and pure
In the eyes of the beholder,
In the hands
Who gave him life,
He's an angel in disguise.

Beholden I am,
For God heard my prayers
Since I can remember
To give me a healthy
Beautiful child.
Beholden I am,
For everything I will do
With him
And everything he will learn
With me.

May 23, 1991

Candles

I light a candle every night
And devotedly pray
For the heavens to hear me
And for help to come quickly
And in full.
I need to protect the child
And fix my life in disarray.
I pray for knowledge,
Guidance, strength,
Patience and bravery
As my enemy
Wants to weaken me
Taking my child
Away from me
And that, shouldn't be.

Through the years,
I made a collection
Of clear and color containers,
From short and beautiful
Edged fancy votive holders
To extra tall glasses
With pictures and prayers
To every saint.
One candle ends
And I light another one.
Candles of every color and size
Light the room and I pray
To the saints and angels,
I make promises and offerings
To bring my enemy down.

I pray day and night,
I pray every moment
I am awake.
Over the candlelight
I pray to God
To keep me upright
As my enemy's mockery
Makes me cry
And weakens my knees.
To keep hope alive,
I light candles for days on end
And the smoke already
Left a dark spot
On the white ceiling.

I pray and pray
And it seems
God is not listening.
On the verge of losing faith,
I changed my strategy
And I began to be a warrior.
I couldn't lose hope
And by the light of a candle,
I began to pray with urgency
For the truth to come afloat,
For the truth to be known.

I light candles
With a renewed hope
And the prayers
Are short, precise
And with the ultimatum
I also live under.
Let the truth come afloat,
Let us be seen
For whom we are,

Who's honest and who lies.
Let the judges judge
By our actions, words
And the truth in our faces.

Soon, as if God
Sprinkled some
Good luck dust over me,
Things began to fall in place
And my prayers
With direct words
Toppled the enemy down.

I learned to fight
For those who I love,
I learned to defend myself
As no one will care
If I go under
Or above the bridge.
I learned to pray
With concise words
And precise thoughts.
I realized
That God wants specifics
In reasons, requests and petitions
Not generalizations
That are overwhelming,
Tiresome and confusing.

December 31, 1999

I
N
N
O
C
E
N
C
E

The best proof
Of our existence
Is through
What we teach
And the inheritance
We leave.
The children
We leave
Keep our trajectory
Or change
The path of their steps
And, sooner or later,
They come to terms
With their origins.

Naturally

Naturally,
The most beautiful
Little thing,
Was born from me,
The most beautiful baby
That I've seen
Comes to my hands.

Naturally,
I cover him
With kisses, hugs
And love.
At first sight,
I fell in love
Of my own child.
I see the most perfect
Little thing
Like God's miracle
And the wonders
Of the nature.

He is cute, quiet
And always smiling,
He responds to my voice
Naturally.
Sometimes,
Even if I laugh
When I talk and sing,
He bursts into tears
Full of sadness.

He senses my sadness
And he gets startled
From any noise
Or activity.
There's no doubt,
The emotions
Are transferred
Before birth
As even if I faked
Happiness,
He was nourished
With love,
Sentimentality
And depression,
Naturally.

June 5, 1991

A Baby

With the soul
Of an angel,
I descended
From heaven above
In cotton diapers
To make someone cry
And laugh in wonder.

I've become restless,
A walking
Mischief-maker,
Strong, wise, and happy,
Beautiful, lovable
And loving.

Perhaps I'll change,
But that must be seen
In each day
I forth live.

May 1, 1992

The Rattle

A rattle hanging
On the supermarket shelves
Caught my eye,
I took the package
Between my hands
To appreciate
The colored beads
That fell
In the spiral within
Releasing a soft sound.

The first little toy,
The only rattle
My baby had,
Fed my dreams.
I found encouragement
In that rattle
To improve myself,
It gave me hope
That things will be better.

How beautiful my baby
Will look
Playing with the rattle
I bought him with so much love.

May 1, 1990

Teddy Bear

A teddy bear,
No matter the size,
Shape, or color,
No matter
How it looks,
Is always
Nice to have
When you're blue.

A teddy bear,
No matter
How fluffy or soft,
No matter
How old,
Is the comfort
For your broken soul.

A teddy bear
Doesn't ask
And doesn't respond,
Just listens
To your comments.
A teddy bear—
Once you see it,
You'll know,
You lead,
He'll follow,
No matter
Where you go.

A teddy bear,
Your loyal friend
For sharing
Smiles and tears,
Sighs and screams.
A teddy bear
Is to love
And hug and kiss,
And at times
To punch and seize.

A teddy bear
Opens your heart
To kindness
And all things.
A teddy bear
Makes you strong,
Makes you brave,
No matter
If you're alone,
No matter
If you're in the dark,
A teddy bear
Holds you up
And lets you explore
The gifts of life.

October 7, 1997

Santa Claus

On Christmas Day,
At twelve midnight,
Santa arrives
In his sleigh
Loaded with toys
To cheer
Girls and boys.

On December 24,
Children sleep
With one eye open,
One eye closed,
Trying to catch
Santa Claus
Making a move.
But if he sees
You're awake,
He'll make you dream.
That, I will bet!

Santa Claus
Brings happiness
To everyone around
Just by ringing his bells.
His laughter, '*Ho, ho, ho,*'
Is very distinguished.
Oh, that beautiful sound
Leaves an echo
When he's out.
Those who believe,
Listen, and behave
Feel Santa Claus

Arrive each December
If their actions
Are good
And sincere
When they share.

November 5, 1997

Kisses And Hugs

Kisses and hugs
For the one I love.
A hug
To share my warmth;
A kiss
To share my dreams.

Hugs and kisses,
Always available,
Always in demand,
Always given
To fill the senses
And calm the complaints.

September 25, 1999

The Outcome

Although my child
Doesn't know
His own father,
There is great resemblance
Between them.
The child has
The same shape of eyes,
The shape of the face,
The same way of talking,
The same kind of laughter,
He scratches his chin
And does so many things
In the same way
As if they saw each other daily
And he copied the gestures.

It amazes
And pleases me
To see how natural
Is the outcome of the bloodline
And how incredible
Are the strong characteristics
Of inheritance.

July 3, 1994

A Dad

My child
Barely articulates
How he feels
And what he thinks
But he wants me
To buy him a dad
From the K-Mart store.

Innocent child he is,
He can't explain
The reasons
But he knows
What he's missing
And what everyone else has.
In his short life
He feels the abandonment
And the emptiness
That the father leaves
When he's absent.

The innocent child
Sees the other children
Full of joy and excitement
When their father arrives
And the often remind him
Their dad is not his
And the child's smile
Starts to disappear.
He's living what I have lived.

September 17, 1994

Tenderness

My beautiful child
Was born to bring joy,
Tenderness and affection.
He awakes each morning
Smiling and talking
And he brightens my day.

My beautiful child
Approaches people
And follows anyone
With no worries or fears.
He's caring and tender,
He asks and talks,
He hugs who is near.

My love for him never ends,
His love for me is shown daily
By patting my face
With excitement and love,
His kisses and hugs
Are constant
And doesn't let go of my hand.
Such happiness it is
To have created such tender being,
God awarded me with him.

October 23, 1993

A Child

With the soul of an angel,
A child, a baby,
Descends from the heavens.
In cotton diapers dressed
And given as a precious gift
That satisfies the heart.

A child to love
For all eternity.
Beautiful, like love itself,
A child is special
And, in many ways, is unique.

A baby born of love:
That's what my child is.
Pride of my home
And pride of my being,
Heir of my emotions,
Reason for my sacrifice.
My child:
The greatest proof
I walked this earth.

October 6, 1997

Sunshine

The birth of my child
Brought me back to reality
And brought me back to life.
With his presence alone,
My baby brings the sunshine
Into my heart.
With his smiles
And his little laughter,
The sun enters in my house
Through any and all
Windows and doors.

I feel hope
And contentment,
Bliss, pride and positivity,
Self-trust and strength,
Optimism and dreams
Just looking at him.
I found new determination
For self-improvement
And to be the best mother
The child deserves.

I never thought a tiny person
Would make me feel so rich
But my greatest accomplishment
And the biggest treasure I have
Is giving life to the child
Who, in turn, gave me life
At his birth,
And now I feel complete.

I never thought
I could love someone so much,
I am so glad
We can laugh at the silly stuff
Because my baby
Is my sunshine,
My cloudy day,
My thunderstorm
And my snowy day.
He's everything
And does everything
That changes my mood,
And to make him laugh,
I tell my baby
He is my Sunny Delight
And sometimes
He's my Hawaiian Punch too.

May 25, 1994

Warrior

My baby was born a warrior
With a beautiful face,
Loving attitude
And kind heart
But behind the big smiles
And contentment,
He has a strong grip
And strong slamming fist.

In his sweet soft voice,
He's strong minded,
Stubborn and hard headed
Who loves to argue
And give his opinion
Even if he's not asked.

He loves to practice
The super hero actions
From the Power Rangers
And, sometimes,
With no warning,
His baby fat
Comes down crushing
With the knee dive
Learned from wrestling
Mixed with karate moves.
All this comes out
Of his little body
While trying to do his moves
And exclaiming sounds,
1,2,3, go! Yaah!

He doesn't meddle
In anyone's problems
But in his little mind,
He tries making peace
With his argument
When the words from Moses,
He-Man, and Jurassic Park,
All come together
With what he's learned
In the Boys Scouts
And the power
He thinks it has given him
To defend family
Against the neighbor.
He screams and argues,
'No fighting. Stop fighting.
I say no fighting …
I have the power.
I am in the Boys Scouts!
I say, I have the power!
Shoot them! …
And let my people go.'

No doubt about it,
My son is practicing
To be a hero
And save the day
And those in need
But while he masters his moves,
The teddy bears
Will be his punching bag
And soft cushiony rug.

August 5, 1995

24

ADHERENCE

Extra things,
Extra emotions
And extra words
But with special meaning
All comes to mind
And all comes from living.

A Mother Cries

A woman cries
From impotence and pain
Listening to the reprimands
From the man
Who says to love her.
She cries alone
And in his presence
For not being as he wishes.
The spark is alit
And she's reduced to nothing
With his finger on her face,
His insults and screams
That never end.

A woman cries
Left alone, empty handed
In a silence that befuddles
In the darkness of the home
When the man she loves
Spoke ill of her.
Pretending to suffer,
He escapes with his new lover
To start a new life
Full of lies and grievances.

A woman cries
Amid the depression
That keeps her
In an immobile state.
In the process of grieving,
It seems she cries
For a love that died

Although the man
Is still alive.

A mother
Spends the nights crying
Seeing her child
Doesn't have the love
From his father,
She doesn't understand
How the man can turn his back
On the innocent child
Who needs everything.

A mother cries
When she faces the negligence
From a family that is corrupt
When they delay
Giving the attention
And care for the child
Only to cover up
For the scoundrel, miserable
And rude adult man.

A mother cries
Seeing the man demand
For custody to satisfy
His whim and vengeance
From the child support
He pays.
The judge, without questions
Or wanting to hear comments
Of the facts or what is denied,
Granted visitation rights.
The authority decides
And the child is thrown
Into a house

With people he doesn't know
And where there's no love,
Patience or compassion for him.

A mother cries and pleads
To the authorities
They return her child
But the authorities don't see
Or listen the injustices
That lies present in the eyes
And the wickedness
And mockery
Coming out of the mouth.

The mother suffers
The disillusion of the judges
Not seeing the monster
Inside the negligent man
Who comes smiling
Joined by a woman
Who's his shadow;
He's charismatic
Like the devil
And the woman
Is charming like a witch.
They're good actors
And have everyone fascinated
With the stories they tell.

I am that mother
Who has cried enough.
For a time,
Everything was against me.
It was two against one,
She was the brain
That thinks and plans

And he was the body
That obeys and performs.
They wanted my child
To not pay the child support
And they wanted to see me
Six feet under,
In prison or in the asylum
But I am pleased to know
I put an end to that episode.

I am that mother
Who has suffered enough.
I prayed to God
For so many things, many times
And it seemed
He wasn't listening
And I saw myself alone
Defending my child
With sword and cloak
And defending myself
In the same manner.
The accusers
Were like buzzards
Waiting for me to fall.
With time
The truth came afloat,
Some got their punishment,
– I got my son.

June 5, 1999

Little Bird

My dying little bird,
Wounded in its cage,
Bleeding from its wings,
You wish to free yourself,
If only they'd let you.

Your chirping, your color,
And your fluffing are all gone.
My little bird has been plucked.
The warmth was denied to you,
And you die of hunger and thirst.
No one comes to see you.

Silly little bird,
You nested
In a forbidden place.
With your chirping
You cheered some hearts,
But they were ungrateful
Wretched people.
Rest on me.
I'll heal your wounds,
Wounds that close
But are not forgotten.

March 10, 1991

My Pillow

My loyal mate
Of nothing complains
And nothing says.
My pillow
Captures the tears
Of my relief
And feels the smiles
When, mischievous,
The mind dreams.

My pillow,
With no heart or face,
To my confessions
Is always attentive,
Listens to my laments
With interest
When my emotions
Release me.

My pillow—
I throw it off
Or embrace it
As I find it convenient.
It conforms to my body
With no criteria,
Rejection or blame.

My pillow,
It's the support when I write
And on paper I leave my tears.
It also reassures me
When I take my anger out
In my dreams.

My pillow,
The best friend of my life.
I ask her questions,
And in dreams
I get the answers.

December 13, 1997

The King

The man self-crowns
As king of his home
And neither poverty
Nor lack of education
Keeps him from imposing
Authority as he pleases.

The wife and children
Become his loyal servants
Controlled and dominated
By a strong hand
Of unpredictable violence.
He governs his home
Like a dictator,
Cruel and selfish,
With no pity or laments
But with a touch
Of kindness, tolerance
And decency
That arise for a moment
In front of others.

As a man, he's free
Of criteria and disparagement
Of leaving the home
To make ends meet
Or even having a fling
But at home,
His presence and money
Come as minimal
And are given
Like an act of charity.

In his sporadic
And rushed visits,
Just to follow tradition,
The family shows
Order, silence, respect
And obedience to the man
They no longer know.
He comes back home
Certain to find
Appreciation for his work
But only finds silence
And indifference
From the children
Who didn't get
His time or affection.

In the monotonous routine,
He dreams the good life
In the rolling hills
And open fields
But, in a moment's notice,
In an outburst of anger
Against the mate,
The children
Come to her defense.
The children grew up
And are no longer so meek,
The wife is not so weak
And she's no longer the dummy
In the man's rough hands.
There is now autonomy
In the palace
And self-defense
Against the tyranny
Of the ruler king.

The king finds
His despotism
Is no longer tolerated
And makes excuses
To escape the kingdom
That's turning against him.
Deceiving everyone,
He walks away like a criminal
From the only life
He's ever known.

The uprooted king
Remained in faraway lands
But warns and threatens
The mate she'll pay dearly
If she's disloyal to him.
In secret,
He makes another home
And, as it tends to happen,
He commits
All the sins and failures
He hated, warned and judged
On his children
But he makes others
To be the villain,
Hides his hand
And cries of how he's treated.

The man who had a palace
Now has nothing,
The man who was a king,
Now has no crown,
No mate and no children.
The man who ruled,
Now has no power.
Now he looks like a beggar

With no power or defenses.
He's alone
And now buys his company,
Support and intermediaries
With a few coins.
But that's the way it is,
Those who live ruling
And leave by deceiving,
Live alone and in ruins.

December 26, 1999

Frozen

Summer
Was confounded
With autumn
And autumn
Soon gave way to winter
And winter comes
Among the dry leaves
With a sense
Of internal solitude
And the airs of sadness leak
Through the windows
And crevices.

Winter came early
With the vengeance
Of collecting
For the tempered weather spells
In the Central Valley.
Winter brought
Waves of cold
And freezing gusts
And, at a distance,
I see snow in the mountains
Of the Sierra Nevada
And the hills to the coast.
Nice surprise
And beautiful sight,
Days before Christmas,
The Central Valley
Got a nice blanket of snow.

January brought us
Another surprise;
Waves of intense cold
That hurt to the bones
And the continuous
Freezing days
Caused the water
In the fountains to freeze
And the pond where I saw
The ducks swimming,
Is where they now walk,
Slip and shiver.

The big freeze
Broke the water pipes
And destroyed many homes
And caused accidents
On the roads.
No one was safe
From the effects
Of the big freeze.
Snow falls
On the valley once
In a decade or two.
Although it was historic,
I wasn't prepared.
I didn't have a camera
To photograph the scenery.
I have no pictures
Of the events
When my baby
Was about to be born.

March 2, 1991

Interlock

Spring and summer
Are confounded by the greenery
And fall and winter
Turned into one season.
Winter came early
And remained for a long time,
The change of weather
Doesn't show up.

The scenery
Doesn't change much
When the sight is foggy
And the view is blocked.
It seems the weather
And the scenery
Are interlocked
With my fragile emotions.
It seems the scenery is dull
When I cannot see
Farther than my pain,
It seems the weather
Knows what I feel
And wants to join
My exhaustion.

March 20, 1992

Bees

Floral perfumes
In spring or summer
Attract birds and also bees.
The bees don't know
If the smell
Is from a scented bottle
Or the flowers in bloom.
They chase and chase
Until they land
On the skin, the clothes
Or the hair.

Perhaps the bees
Don't want to bother us
And mistake
Where to stop
But the buzzing
Is closer and closer,
Is heard on the ears,
Is felt on the neck,
Is felt flying very near,
And the hair is shaken,
Fingers slide
Through the long strands
And one bee is seen fly off
Then another one comes out
To catch up with the first.

April 30, 1994

El Niño
(The weather)

Rain comes soft
And in storms,
Continuous and heavy,
And, just as it is good,
So it is also bad
As from so much rain
The sight gets foggy.
On the streets,
Unaware of the risk ahead,
I gave a wrong step
That made me fall
In the flooding street
Just feet from my door.

The storms flooded
My neighborhood
And I fall in the puddle of water
Mixed with trash,
Dirt and twigs.
I can't stand up
Not getting any more wet
But from down there,
I see my mother,
With her broken arm,
And my young son
Unable to help me.

The sprinkles
Are coming stronger
And I heard myself
Speak forcefully and angrily,

'Why do you cry?
Instead of crying
Help me get up.'
It made me angry
To see my mother's tears
Of helplessness.
Although
She offered her hand,
I got up on my own.
I always find a way
To get up and out
And not remain
Stagnant like the water.

April 25, 1997

Beneficence

Help arrives
But not graciously
Neither by handfuls.
Some people count the times
They offered help
And others count the bills
They put on the table.

It's hard not to see
That it takes a strong
And energetic voice
To make them pay attention
So they understand
The gravity of the problem
That consumes the mind,
Emotions and life
For the one in trouble.

The offers, the dollar bills
And the words of support
Are given with claims.
The help is given
But with warnings,
Reprimands, criteria
And selfish opinions.
As they not see themselves
In this situation or in these shoes,
It hurts them
To take out the bills
And make an act of beneficence.

The help is clearly
An act of beneficence
That's given
Like to the unknown beggar
On the streets
And the charity is accepted
With pain from the need.

Those who give charity
Don't see that poverty
Is lack of resources
And visual obstruction.
Poverty and need
Bring out the lack of pride
And lack of integrity
To say, '*No thanks*',
And not accept the help
That, frankly,
Is not given graciously.

November 27, 1999

Gatherings

Not all gatherings
Are good, nice,
Fun, appropriate
Or wanted.
We see each other often
But being all together
Causes tears
In the familial fabric,
And pressures, anger,
Arguments and hurt feelings
Make someone cry
Then there's precipitation
To flee from them.

Gatherings are dreaded
As someone ends up losing
In the moment
Of clearing things up,
The attacks are
For what is said or done,
For the tone of voice
And the facial expressions
That arise naturally.
Everything is inspected
And analyzed
And end up for later
In the list.

The unwise, weak and meek
Learned to be silent
And move aside
So the verbal blows

Don't hurt as much.
Sometimes we keep neutrality
In the topics discussed
To avoid enemies.
Sometimes we keep the face
Of indifference
To not end up angry,
Offended
Or with the soul crushed
As things are said and done to us.

Sometimes,
We attend the gatherings,
Not out of desire,
But out of obligation,
Or commitment
Or to quiet down the critics.
So then,
Why the welcoming
With hugs and kisses
If we then fight
Like dogs and cats
With so much ire?

December 28, 1994

Miseries

Burdensome it is
To face the endless poverty,
To see the dust
The shoes pick up
On the streets with no asphalt,
And see that, on the shadows
And in the light,
The dust circulates, falls
And adorns the tables and floors.

I felt an immense sadness,
Anguish and impotence
To see the little dirty faces
Asking for charity
With their saddened eyes.
Difficult was
To see a mother barefooted
With her legs ashy
From the sticky dust
And her feet wounded
From the harmful objects
Found at every step.
It was even worse
To see the child in her arms
With old clothes
Inadequate for winter
And crying from hunger.

The mother raised her hand
Asking for charity
Near the traffic
But no one stopped,

No one gave her a cent,
Everyone went by in a rush
Ignoring their presence,
Ignoring the dried-up tears
On her colorless
And emaciated face
And ignoring the child
Who's unable to see
From the continuous weeping.

I lowered my head
And I shed some tears
In silence
For her and for me.
I wanted to give her
All and more
For the great sadness
She provoked in me.
I wanted to help her
For the pain I saw she carried
And I gave her
The coins I had in my wallet.
But, what good can
Some coins bring
When hunger and need
Come from so long past?
How I wished to find
So many dollar bills
To make her rich
But I had nothing on me.

I wanted to cry the sadness
Stuck in my throat
Looking at so much misery
And being unable to help her.
I wanted to cry openly

But I held it in,
She doesn't need pity,
She deserves compassion
And acts of beneficence
To be given graciously.

I knew poverty
Has many levels
As, even in poverty,
There's honor and status.
Some have more than others
And others have nothing at all
But hunger abounds
Among the poor.
How sad and shameful
That God
Did not distribute
Riches and justice equally.
He gave all to some
And left most others
With their mouths open.
How disgraceful it is
That in any terrain,
Circumstances or facts
Misery unites us
As our hunger and need
Has us stuck
To those who boast
Of the mercy given
And don't take in account
The suffering they've caused.

December 19, 1995

DEDICATIONS

Some people
Leave strong prints
And they deserve respect
For the memories
And the admiration
Of who they were
And what they motivated.

Diana

A Sleeping Beauty
She now is
And forever is laid to rest.
Her beauty and wit
Charmed the world
Throughout the years.
She was a princess
And a lady indeed,
Wherever she was.

Living in a bad marriage
Of lies and treason,
She lived in a prison
Guarded by the authority
Of the palace.
Diana was her name,
And the world made her
The Princess of the People
When she showed love,
Respect and empathy
To those in need.

She was tied to her title
That limited her words,
Actions and distance.
Followed she was
Wherever she went,
She found no space
To breathe freely.
One night in August,
The persecution became fatal.

Such a shame,
She's gone at a young age.
If she wasn't happy,
If she was pressured,
Now she has time and space
To open up her wings.
In the heavenly palace,
She'll have the peace
She wished.

The fairy tale
Never existed
But her life
Came to a sad ending.
It's a great loss
No one can conceive,
The world has shed tears
Over this tragedy.
No one will replace her.
I know, she was unique.

Goodbye, Diana,
Princess of Wales.
Farewell to the woman
Who captivated our hearts.
Your legacy will go on,
And the memories of you
Will forever live.

September 1, 1997

Thanks

To my doctor

Thanks for listening,
Thanks for your patience,
Thanks for your words
Of encouragement.

Some have done some,
Others have done less,
And others
Have done a bit more,
But you have done enough
To make me know
I can go on.

Hopefully the circle
Of caring for others
And being appreciated
Never stops.
Good luck
Wherever you are.

June 4, 1996

Blue Eyes

A handsome man
With beautiful blue eyes,
White skin, a good heart
And so many dreams
Came to me.
He kept me company,
Listened to my stories
With interest,
He made me feel special
And lifted my spirits
With his encouragement
And flattery.
He was my friend
But when I heard his words
And I saw his love for me
In his eyes,
I gave him a chance.

His touch was tender
And his kiss was soft,
He was quiet and respectful,
He was sweet and gentle,
I had everything at hand,
Nothing to demand,
Nothing to request
But I wasn't pleased.
His lifestyle, dreams
Visions and pleasures
Were so different to mine.
I could not relate
And my mind often wandered
On what was out there.

Years later,
Another story,
Another chance,
Another handsome man,
With white skin
And beautiful blue eyes,
Came to me
Asking to be my friend
And, perhaps even more.
Although I was taken,
He didn't settle
At being an acquaintance.
He was kind, sociable,
Talkative, giving, and helpful.
He wanted to win
My attention and my heart
And did much
Just to know me.

As a single woman,
He kept me company
In my most vulnerable moments.
He listened to my pain
And showed me he cared.
He was willing,
Happy and ready
To take on the responsibility
Others had rejected
But I couldn't bring myself
To loving him.
I wanted to respond
To the warmth he offered
And I tasted those lips,
I felt that embrace
But I did not feel safe
And my mind

Was comparing
The before and after effects.

In my mind,
Every difference
Seemed to be a barrier,
Every similarity
Lacked something
That was halting me
From falling in love
With either one of them
And I couldn't see myself
Being part of their dream.
In my mind,
Fears and worries
Made me curtail
The relationships
Right from the inception.

Two men,
Two options discarded,
Two chances
Never appreciated or taken,
Two times love
Was trimmed at the start,
Two times life
Was giving me
A chance at love,
Two times I couldn't see
Or understand
That I was losing a good man
From my foolish interest
In someone
Unworthy of my love
Who never loved me.

But, after all
Is said and done,
I wonder, from time to time,
How my life could've been
If I had accepted
Either one of them.

Love is a selfish thing.
We become relentless
In pursuing a relationship
With the one we love
Hoping to be loved back,
Believing the challenge
And the chase
Would have a reward,
At the same time,
We are ruthless,
Inconsiderate and oblivious
When we completely
Set aside, ignore, reject
And then deny
Those who love us
With no problem at all.

December 20, 1999

In Memory of Violeta

The sleeping child
Will wake no more.
In a profound sleep she remains,
And now rests in peace.

Like a new flower,
They pulled her life away.
And we can only mourn
For the great loss
That left us
With the cruelty of life.

The pretty child,
The good child,
With her innocence
And suffering,
She earned heaven.
It hurts me to see
She's no longer here,
I am relieved to know
That in the voyage
She now takes
No one can hurt her any more,
Since the angels
Take her by the hand
Onto the path
The Lord dictated for her.

My eyes will see you no more.
My hands will touch you no more.
My ears will hear you no more.
My lips will not tell you again

That I love you.
But I am comforted to know
I did my best for you.
And through the memories,
Never will you die.

April 7, 1995

You're Gone

You're gone,
And now that you are
With the Lord
I know you suffer no more.

It's too late
To tell you I love you.
It's too late
To wish for anything.
You're gone to heaven
And my pain has no end.

I took it for granted
The time, your presence
And your teachings
But now that you're gone,
They became important.
You will never die.
You live in my memories,
Through the things
You left behind,
Through the songs,
Through the pictures,
Through everything,
Old and new,
Everything has a touch of you.

I am so sorry
For everything I did
Or didn't do.
Please, give me a sign,
Show me you're there,

And that I'm not alone.
I miss you every minute
Of every day
And I often call out
Your name.
I feel your spirit
As if you were
My guardian angel
And I feel you near.

February 18, 1995

Reminiscence

My college days
Was a new beginning
But the excitement in others
Was discouragement,
Fear and anxiety for me.
Everyone was a stranger
And acted so sophisticated
And I felt I was left behind
In every aspect.
Everyone had someone
To share their free time
And I had no one.
Anxiety set in
And I wanted to escape
But I had nowhere to go
If I only walk with purpose
And direction.

My first friend
Came on an early
September day
With a well ironed shirt
And a red scarf
Hanging from his pants.
He became a good friend,
He kept me company
On Friday afternoons
When the campus
Was deserted.
He was respectful, artistic,
Affectionate and talkative.
He easily drew roses

And gave them to me
As giving away
A bouquet of flowers.
He called me 'Sweetheart'
And held my hand
To kiss it so delicately
When I measured the inches
He was allowed to touch.

My next friend
Always had a smile on him
And was very sociable,
He wore super big glasses
But had the look
Of a good young man.
He was into teaching
But dreamt of being an actor,
He motivated
And promoted optimism
And good character.
He was determined
To finishing what he started,
He was a leader
And organizer
And we followed his plans.

Another friend
Had dark skin, kinky hair
And damaged rough hands,
He was into teaching
And loved folkloric dancing.
He was a good listener,
Quiet and serious,
We had an appointment
To socialize every morning
Before there were any listeners

Or interference.
It was easy to talk to him
And time went by so fast
Talking of everything
And nothing at all.

A friend with tanned skin
Showed off
His developing muscles
Through the cropped T-shirts.
It was obvious
He enjoyed my approval
And led my hand
To touch his strong
And solid arms.
And just for pleasure,
I called him Mr. America
And, in return,
He called me Miss Universe.
With him,
It was short talks
Very enjoyable
And full of laughter.

A friend, totally different
From the others,
Was tall, blue-eyes
And cowboy at heart.
He was a man of few words
But so smart
And focused on the stars.
I felt inadequate
For not understanding
Nor appreciating
The beauty and mystery
Of space and the planets.

A beautiful friend
Had white round face
Like the moon
And her black eyes
Made me feel understood,
She made me feel safe
And protected.
We shared life stories
And she understood
My weak points
And made me strong
In other ways.
Other friends called me
'The Cover Girl'
But she called me,
'Miss L'Oreal'
And that was a great feeling.

I nicknamed a friend,
'Votive,' as it related
To her name and height
And she also took it very well
When, observing her, I said
She sneezed like a cat.
She was also funny
But in a serious way,
She was understanding,
Patient, kind,
And a very good helper.
She supported
And encouraged me
And when I complained
Of other's comments,
She made gestures
As to not to pay attention.

I wanted to be like her
As it seemed nothing
Brought her down,
Nothing bothered her
And nothing got her mad
But when I sensed
She was in trouble,
I made her my roommate
To help her out
And we were two fighting
What's lurking around.

A peculiar friend
Dressed up
Like Boy George
And in a small town,
She gave lots to talk about
But she didn't care,
She was happy and proud.
I liked her indifference
To the comments.
I'm not sure how we met
But she was a good listener,
Talkative, funny,
Helpful, giving,
Understanding and attentive.
She loved to share stories
And I shared mine.
She made me laugh
When she often said
Not to understand the stories
Of 'my many men.'

Girl and guy friends
Trusted me
And I trusted them,

They gave me
Their attention
Respect and affection,
They looked for me
And wanted my company.
They made me feel special,
Loved and important,
My self-esteem
Went from the ground
To the heavens so quick,
I felt on top
And at the center,
Like salt and condiments.

New students came later
And I experienced a time
Of envy, jealousy,
Sadness, and anger
Because, with their manners,
And, in a thousand ways,
These girls
Were displacing me.
They were removing me
From my position
As they seized the attention
That I had earned.

Some of my friends
Gave them the time
For the moment,
But for serious talks,
Advice and opinions
They looked for me
And that, made me happy
And kept me satisfied.

Looking back,
I am happy to know
That I helped some people
And they got the attention
I got from them.
Being honest with myself,
I also know
I made some people
Mad for silly reasons
But I was too young
And ignorant
To understand
The silliness of things,
But now I apologize
For the senseless conflicts.
I also know I offended
And I hurt
People's feelings
Although unintentionally,
But to see
Their faces change
From my blundering words,
Made me sad
As it hurt me too
And I am so sorry
For the pain I inflicted.

With all the good
And all the bad
Of my young adult life,
These were my best years.
So many friends,
So many incidents
And characters,
So many beautiful words
And tokens of affection

Stamped in my mind
That, even today,
I smile as I remember.
I miss the kisses on my hand
And being called '*Sweetheart*,'
I miss the optimism
And encouraging words,
I miss the discreet
Compliments
That made me feel good
About myself
Because I had great friends
And they all left a big mark
In my memories.

Wish I would go back
In time,
I'd make better choices
And I'd correct
What I did wrong,
I'd give everyone
A chance equally
With respect and affection.
Wish I'd kept in touch
With everyone
To know what became
Of my dear school friends.
Wish I had kept
Pictures of each one
To know it was not a fantasy
What I lived, who I met
And what I remember,
And just as important,
To know that I was loved.
Wish I would tell them
How important they were

And how I miss them all.
Memories go wrapped
In a sigh
Filled with good wishes
And the question,
Where did time go?

By graduation day,
They all had a vision
Of their future,
They all knew the route
Of their path
And I feel I remained idle
In the question mark.
Nothing remains
Of that sociable, happy,
And opinionated woman
That I was.
Today, I see that woman
In the third person
And only feel her
Like a dream.

September 6, 1998

Teresa

I ended up alone
In the confusion
Of my confinement
And the turmoil
Of the loneliness and silence.
But my saving came
In the form
Of a pretty young woman
With big green eyes
Named Teresa.
She had a genuine smile
And her positivity
Was contagious.
She seemed to understand me
And gave me the support
And attention
That my mind needed
To feel strong and content.

Teresa kept me company
Through all my social,
Mental and moral tribulations.
She always had time
And showed interest
In listening to my problems
And never complained
Of my befuddling words,
Never complained
That the topic, the problem
Or my conclusions
Were repetitive.

She helped me see
My accomplishments
And raised my self-esteem
When I was blinded
By negativity.
She gave me the sanity
Amid my conflicts
And gave me the strength
To keep on fighting.
I owe her so much,
I know Teresa
Gave me a hand
In a thousand ways.

I didn't see it then
But the person
I least expected
Became my best friend,
The very best friend
I needed at the time
And if I was given a choice,
I'd choose Teresa
Time and time again
To be my best friend
In my time of conflict.

May 28, 1998

REFLECTIONS

There is inspiration
Everywhere I go.
If I take time to reflect,
I find there is meaning
In everything.

If I awaken the senses,
I see there is magic
And grandeur
In my surroundings
And sadness, too,
Has its worth.

The Aftermath

Not everything
Is learned in school,
Books or classes,
Sometimes,
The most impactful lessons
Are learned out on the streets.

So long after
My school years, I say
I haven't learned enough.
I didn't see that people
Hide their behavior,
Emotions, temper and desires
Like a big secret
Only waiting to let it out
At the precise chance
When they have the upper hand.
I learned in my own flesh
That the most important lessons
Are learned instantly
And they're argued
And analyzed
In the aftermath.

So many books,
Lectures and sessions,
So many years
In the classroom,
But I didn't learn
How to discern
The interactions in life.
In the aftermath,

Of little to no knowledge,
On preventing violence,
Only meditation, wishing
And regrets remain.

Wish I'd learn
How to distinguish
A relationship
That is long lasting
To one that's momentary.
I should've learned
How to identify
A sexist man,
Who comes and envelops us
With their lies
And identify the aggressive
And traitor man
With the face of a victim
Blaming everyone freely
But doesn't accept
Responsibility.

To prevent, protect
And defend myself,
They should've taught me
How to distinguish
The chronic explosive
Temperament
And selfish violent behavior
That comes with it.
They should've taught us
How get rid
Of the possessive, controlling
Manipulative man
Before it's too late.

I should've learned
To see ahead of me
And analyze my past too
So I can see
When the mistakes
Were made.
They should've taught me
To use my eyes
And see my life as it is
And what's to come.
I could've seen
How a man lifted me up
But, at the same time,
Kept me down.
I could've known
That by pleasing him,
I became a recluse
And my loneliness became
An emotional setback
Which made me vulnerable,
Fragile and needy
And I was the perfect thing
For the next monster
Who saw the advantages.

In the aftermath,
Of not studying
The social behavior,
Not studying the mind,
Then, keeping ignorance alive
By not asking questions
Or saying anything
For fear or shame,
And by lacking the advice
And oversight,
I repeated

The same mistake twice.
However, time and experience
Gave me the vision
And the getaway
Of a life with no life.
I was able to see the man,
Blackmailer and manipulative,
Who came to be
Worse than the first mistake.

All in all,
My college education
Gave me the smarts
And the ideas
To defy the system.
It also helped me
Defend myself,
With teeth and nails
From the cad of a man,
Evil and selfish,
Who was destroying
The sprout of my tree.
Not everyone is lucky
At loving and being loved
So for me,
It's better to be alone
Than suffer a relapse.

December 30, 1999

Advice

To be loved
And respected,
Love yourself first.
If you wish to love others,
Respect, protect, defend
And care for yourself,
Be nice to yourself,
And don't allow anyone
To mistreat you
Or disrespect you.
Your spouse is your equal
And is your mate.
Remember, your light
Is in your inner strength.

Respect yourself
With words and actions.
Respect others,
And you will get
The attention you deserve
For the goodness of your life
And not for the frivolous
Things you do.

Communicate
With your conscience,
With your body,
And with your senses.
Your own best friend
And your first doctor is you.
The time and attention
You give your body and mind

Are worthwhile
In positivity and health.

Accept yourself
As you are,
Be happy
With what you got.
Physical traits
Are only superficial.
No one is like you
And only your spirit
Has a special place in life
And your life is essential
To the time and place
That you occupy.

Admire your work,
Feel good
About what you create,
It should be your ability,
Cognizance
And of your choosing.
We all have
Talents and skills,
We just need to search
What we like
To know what fits right.
Do not be your worst critic
As others
Do it for you already
But remember
To improve in all things.

To live peacefully,
Free yourself
From the afflictions

Of the past,
Let go of the pain
And resentment
That take you nowhere
And you gain nothing
By holding to that.
In relationships,
As much as you try,
Nothing will ever be
Clear enough, resolved
Or forgotten
So don't live
Over-analyzing
People or the incidents.
To live broken
Is to please
Those who hurt you.

Think before doing
Or saying anything,
You don't want to offend
Or hurt anyone
As things come back
To hunt us down.
Act cautiously but decidedly,
And be strong,
As life doesn't wait
And accept the outcome
Of your decisions.

Be kind, compassionate
And peaceful,
Share the wealth
Of your knowledge
And presence
And it will come back to you

In a thousand ways.
Remember that
Everything you do
Has consequences.

Selfishness and neglect
Make people walk away
So make time
For relatives and friends.
Help them
In their problems and times,
Friendship is built
With little things
And big favors.

Trust yourself,
Build dreams
In your future-to-be.
The dreams of your life
Will be achieved
By your hand
But don't forget
To ask for
And accept help.
Remember, don't listen
To negative criticism
If people don't bring
Anything constructive.
No one lives your life
And they don't know
What you need.

January 17, 1997

Virginity

Losing your innocence
Changes the body and mind,
Being in a relationship
Changes the mood,
Self-esteem and perspectives.
A good relationship
Makes you feel protected,
And averts all fears,
It's easy to get accustomed
To the idea of being in love
And being loved,
It's easy to get accustomed
To the words of affection,
To the embraces,
To the stolen kisses
And the attention given.

And when it ends,
A feeling of inferiority
And insignificance remains,
And an immense solitude,
A huge void, a deep hole,
A gap, deep and wide
Like the abyss,
Is felt and I only see
That I am alone on this side
Of the barbed wire fence
And the entire world
Is on the other side.

And in that solitude,
I dream, I wish,

I yearn, I need,
For a moment, at least,
To have the attention
Of a man
In a glance, in a compliment,
A cordial greeting, a smile,
A word directed to me,
A brush of his fingers
On my hand,
A something
To tell me I am not dead.

But I walk alone
In a deserted city
Even if I am surrounded
By diverse people,
I walk like a lost soul
Even if I have purpose,
Direction, objective
And destiny.
I walk alone and I hide well
My needs and secrets
But I feel a fire
That burns me within
And I see in several men
A possible chance
And I imagine things
I shouldn't do.

Unconsciously,
I look for someone's attention,
Doesn't matter who,
But they're all busy
And they don't see me.
No one asks of me personally
But they all say

My duty
Is with my child
And, at the end,
I am left as a woman.
How sad,
How disappointing,
How heartbreaking
It is to hear those words
From those who live
A stable life with a mate,
From those who don't know
What loneliness
And lack of affection is
And those
Who don't understand
That I am prisoner
Of my culture and beliefs,
Of the eyes that see me
And hunt me
And the loose tongues
Who judge me.

Days, weeks,
Months and years go by,
And soon after,
It all looks the same
As yesterday,
The only thing
That changes,
Is that my child is bigger,
But, in the coffer
Of my secrets,
Emotional and physical,
Loneliness no longer fits
And, as much as I want it,
I don't get used to

A life of repudiation,
Self-denial
And abandonment.

I still exist, I see, I feel,
I think and wish.
For their strength
And independence,
I admire those who enjoy
Living and being alone
But I envy everyone
Who has a mate
For the company,
The affection and support
That I don't have.

One of many days,
A man arrived at my door,
His eyes fixed on me,
Discretely seducing me
With his looks.
He flatters me,
He smiles so happily,
He tells me I am beautiful,
He admires my wits,
And makes me smile.

The compliments,
That were superficial,
Become more intimate
And direct.
I hold back wanting to prevent
The mistakes of the past
But his persistence
Makes me see
The upstanding man

Good family man,
As provocateur
And seductive
Who deserves
A second chance.

A casual meeting,
Between talking
And laughing,
He brushes my hands
With his rough fingers
That scratch
My unaccustomed skin.
The initial reaction
Was bewilderment
From the mishap
But, at the same time,
His fingers were like a match
Lighting my skin
And my face blushed
From the burning.

His voice was convincing
Or I let myself
Be convinced,
But he knew exactly
How to manipulate the situation.
In a moment of weakness,
In a moment of blindness,
I got carried away
By the minute
Of selfish reasons,
I let myself be fooled
By the individual
Who's a lying
Rotten scoundrel.

I was gullible
To his words and promises
That had no base.
Nonetheless,
I am to blame,
I am responsible,
I accept that everything
Falls over me.
I let myself be touched,
I let myself be dirtied.
– All the expectations of me,
I forgot.

The years I lived alone
As modest, decent
And self-restrained,
Hoping to find
A respectful man
With whom to do
Things right,
All came to an end.
A second virginity
Of emotional, mental
And physical state,
Was undone in the hands
Of a common man,
Undeserving
And unappreciative,
And that, has no explanation
Or forgiveness.

February 3, 1998

My Gift

Dear Santa Claus,
I only ask
For one gift:
To bring a lover
Into my life
And, with him,
Many smiles.

I ask
That he loves me
In a good way,
To be kind
And attentive.
I am tired of crying.
I am ready
For a new experience.

Santa Claus,
I'm giving you time
To search out
And find
The one I need.
And at Christmas
I can happily open
The surprise
You have prepared
For me.

June 5, 1999

1995

The years come
And go,
Some go fast and unseen
And others remain
Stuck in the memory
For the occurred events.
Some years are visualized
And others are resented
From the pain they left.

The year begins
With the stillness
Of a common winter
Followed by frequent rains
And gales of wind
That flood, drown, destroy
And then dry up the land.

Spring peeks up
With glee, hope and aromas.
The sun warms up
And the fields are full
With flowers and colors.
But the beauty of spring
Fades with the tragedies
That soon arise.
What seems routine,
Peaceful and boring
Is overturned quickly,
The lady of death
Is making its rounds nearby.

Spring, summer and fall
Entangle in the agony
Of death
And the depression it left.
Seems like a nightmare
That doesn't end,
The life of young women
That were friends
Vanish away.
One after the other,
Though in different ways,
Their life is gone,
Regardless.
How worrisome
And saddening it is for me,
Who's next?
When will it end?

Winter arrives
As did spring,
With news and surprises
That don't cease.
To close the year
With a flourish,
The father
Who didn't want
To know my child,
Now asks for full custody
And the judge
Is eager to grant
First visitation on Christmas
And he'd spend the day
With a total stranger.

Definitely,
1995
Brought much anguish,
Problems and disappointments
But it made me face
The cruel reality
That saying, '*I love you,*'
Is not the same
As the showing it.
The judges,
Who are thought as wise,
And the system,
That doesn't intervene or acts
Until it's too late,
Put the child in danger
Not wanting to see
The true face
Of the monster friend.

January 10, 1996

Simplicity Of The Heart

Letters and syllables,
Simple phrases,
Simple verses,
Words heard
And repeated.

Words boggle my mind,
Images run wild,
And I find new ways
Of telling
What I've told before.

The simplicity
Of the heart
Is evident
When it tells
What it feels
In a confession,
A liberation, a relief
To the burdens
Of the soul, the mind,
And the fingers.

And, also,
Whispering voices
Come to me
And speak their stories,
So secretive, so intimate,
So private, so personal,
But so detailed.
They look for comfort,
They want to be heard.

They have
In their hands
And their memories
Strong words
That I have to write down
Their emotions
Before they disappear.

As I listen,
I learn about me.
I realize no one
Is so alone,
Or so different,
Or special, or unique,
Or weak or dumb,
When the views
And feelings
Are valued
And shared
By more than one.
Quietly
I find my voice,
I find my calling,
And I am not letting go.

December 28, 1999

As a child,
I asked God many times,
Why me?
Why am I different?
Why am I not strong?

And I heard
The inaudible words:
'It's not a matter of the body;
It's the strength of the spirit
And of the mind
That moves and makes changes.
Show them what's important!'

Reflections of my life,
That's all there is left.
To go back to the past
And see my actions,
Erroneous or correct,
But either way,
Always of a woman
Decisive and free
In the most intimate way
Of my thoughts.

January 8, 1998

Episodes

Life is in stages of time,
Incidents and characters,
Life is in phases and steps,
Chapters and segments.
The nouns and times
Interpose, correlate, overlap
And interrupt each other
Creating individual
And collective episodes
That intertwine,
Affect and threaten each other.

Don't know
What the future holds
But the men
Of the past and the present
Are suffocating problems,
That persecute, haunt,
Lie and accuse
As if they were God's
Little angels or innocent.
One was my lover
The other one
Wants to be my husband
But both are villains,
Dominant, advantageous
And are my enemies.

The past wasn't idyllic
As I made me believe,
It was only a hallucination
Of time and facts

Distorted by the idea of love
And are two versions
That don't agree.
The present is absurd,
It's a daymare I am living,
It's into everything
And doesn't give me
Time or place
To breathe deeply
But experience
Taught me to be strong
And not to give in.

The man of the past
And the man of the present,
Each one, in their time,
Said they loved me
And the jealousy scenes
Were the best proof.
What was I thinking?
Why did I fell for them?
No doubt about it,
I am gullible and dumb
But they are
Wicked and tricky.

The man of the past
Was good looking
But hid his malice
Amid the kisses,
He became jealous
From rumors
And interferences.
The man of the present
Is ugly in its traits and mind,
He's naturally

Jealous and possessive.
Wanting to erase the past,
He proposes marriage.
From the envy
Of my daydreams,
He wants to take over
My entire life
And lives watching my face,
My every step
And dissecting what I said.
He demands obedience of me
Wanting me weak
And dependent on him
But he says to love me
In spite of my defects.

The man of the past
Left heavy prints
That hurt and affect
When reviewing
And analyzing
The words and actions.
The past still has a grip on me
Like a beast to its prey
But between fear
And weakness,
Escape is achieved
When I recognize
The mental exhaustion
And the desire to live in peace.

The man of the past
Left me a beautiful gift
And now wants to take
The gift away by force
But with his feet well grounded

And, with such weight,
Stumps and manipulates
What bothers him.
The man of the present
Encourages me to not give up
And to, absolutely,
Forget the past.
He gave peace, briefly,
But makes me see
That the person
In front of the mirror
Deserves respect
And to love oneself first.

The man of the past,
Fickle and temperamental,
Made me shrivel
Like a flower made of paper.
The man of the present,
Shamelessly chauvinist,
Impulsive, aggressive,
Manipulative and controlling,
Wants to be into everything.
It's a constant war
And I am a flower
Withering with no fragrance,
Light, air or water.

The man of the past is astute,
Hypocrite and convincing
And I was young and naïve.
The man of the present
Is also astute but selfish
And a worse scoundrel
Than the past
And he doesn't have me

As he wishes.
The man of the past
Had me hoodwinked
With his apologies
And words of love
And I was mistreated
From ignorance, love
And lack of role models
But now in the present,
I defend myself
With teeth and nails.

The man of the past
Lies, blames,
Persecutes and sneers.
He wants to see me
In prison, the madhouse
Or the cemetery.
He's aggressive like an ogre
And he's a charlatan
With no class or dignity.
The man of the present
Wants to keep me isolated,
Hidden or frightened
In silence,
He's violent and impulsive
Like a monster
With that stern look
Of a cruel dictator.
The past and the present
Are so much alike
As if made
From the same old cloth.

The past and the present
Don't fool me anymore,

I stand my ground
And I attack the enemy
Of the past and the present
From every angle I see.
In silence, I plan
The confrontation
With the furies of the past
And the present,
I find the strength
And determination
To carry on
Putting some distance
And time in between.

I don't know
How the man of the future
Will be or if he will arrive
But the illusion
Of a peaceful life
Helps me defeat
My own fears.
The man of my daydreams
Has the attitude and face
I may want,
He's kind and gentle
And it's a wish
For all the promises
Never articulated
But that take me
Wherever I want to go.

The daydream
Gives me the freedom,
Respect, space
And affection I deserve.
The fantasy image

Is a fresh new start,
It doesn't know who
Or what bothers me,
It doesn't want to know
Of any problems
Or any memories
And doesn't make plans
Or promises,
And makes no petitions.

I don't see or feel
That the daydream
Takes advantage
Of my emotional state
To make me fall
In the traps of love
But, like a hero,
He brings me back to life.
The image of the future
Provokes and feeds me
And gives me strength,
Inspiration, independence
And new perspectives.
It brings me smiles,
Dreams and hopes
With a soft voice
And nice words
And I feel like a tree
Always blossoming.

The episodes
Are hallucinations,
Perceptions and visions
That step over each other.
I loved the man of the past
But I despise

The man in the present
And the man of my daydreams
Is yet to be seen.

Episodes of the past,
Present and future
Feed and intertwine
In what each discover.
In my life,
The past, present and future
Have the factors
And components
That make men be men
And I realize I inherited
Beliefs and weaknesses
That don't favor me,
On the contrary,
They benefit the enemy
But in any episode,
Men are just a character
And I am the writer.

October 1, 1999

CRUMBS

The present
Is a crude reality
Where it's applied
What I learned
In the past
And the mistakes
And character
Are corrected
Before taking the last step.

In the present,
Some relationships
Are unworthy,
Not good at all
And not needed.
Some relationships
Demand
And give nothing
But complain of receiving
Only crumbs
When they don't bring
To the table
Anything substantive.

Your Hero

I was your hero,
I was your salvation,
I was your charming prince,
I was your king
And I was your slave
Though it lasted
For a short while,
I didn't complain.

What more
Did you want?
I beg you to love me,
And you play dumb.
I gave you everything —
I gave you my life,
My body,
My soul
And my faith —
But I'm left empty
As you leave quietly.

What did you miss?
If what you asked for
Was all given to you.
I gave you my time,
My affection,
And my attention,
My love was great,
And you gave nothing,
Not even as charity.

You dreamt
Of a Prince charming
From the fairy tales,
You wished for a lover
Who'd make you laugh,
Dream, and sigh,
You prayed for a hero
Who'd come rescue you,
You expected perfection,
And I was everything.

You wanted a prince,
And I fought the battles,
You wanted a king,
And I made you a palace,
I was your hero
And I was your villain
To blame others
And save your dignity.
Without realizing
What I wanted to sow,
I became your slave,
And now you discard me
Like a beggar
And you leave me
Empty-handed.

A word of love
Doesn't hurt anyone,
Or so I thought.
I was wrong,
Everything about me
Offended you.
You lost everything
Nothing mattered to you
And everything hurt me.

All this is heard
From a controlling,
Emotional blackmailer,
And jealous man
Who sees himself as the hero
And sees himself
As the victim
When my point of view is given
But he doesn't see
That the slandering
And self-praising
Is ridiculous and muddling.

November 5, 1996

Men And Women

Men treat women
Like objects,
But demand respect.
They believe
To own everything
But that, is only in their dreams.

I keep firm that men do
What women let them
And in the end,
It's women who command.

Men without women
Don't do and are not much.
Women without men
Are everything and win it all.

Women manage alone
Work, tend the home and children
While men don't even know
Where to start.

Men criticize, undervalue,
And dominate women,
For fear they become
Stronger and greater than them.
This is called discrimination
No matter how you see it.

February 11, 1997

Passing By

So much was lost
When we said goodbye,
You tell me,
But that is not what I say.
Don't blame anyone,
I told you
I was passing by
In your life
And it was only true.

This relationship
Was not love
Or friendship,
Not even attraction.
From my part,
It was the convenience
To make a home
For my child.
From your part,
It was to give the appearance
Of a hurting good man
Who needs to be loved
And that is worse
Because it was a lie.

June 5, 1999

Jealousy

The phone rings,
And no one answers.
Tell me,
Who is calling?
Tell me,
Who awaits for you?

I'm sorry,
At times people play
With the phone
And take the device
So very lightly.

You get beautiful,
Go out,
And return late.
Tell me,
Who is that for?
Who is that coward?

I have dignity
And decency
Whether close or far
From you.
I like to look good,
But no one
Awaits for me.
It's just that time
Goes by so quickly.

You are so insensitive,
So frivolous.
You appear so private,
So mysterious.
Are you always planning
Your next rendezvous?

I'm sorry,
But at times,
The dilemmas fill my head
And prevent me
From being affectionate
And I prefer
My loneliness,
Where no one criticizes,
Where no one scolds.

I kiss you; I caress you,
And you keep quiet,
Looking thoughtful,
I make love to you,
And you don't respond,
I give everything,
And you offer nothing,
Tell me,
In whose arms
Do you get satisfied?
Tell me,
What is it that you do?

I think of everything
In our lives,
But I've learned
To keep my thoughts quiet
If everything I say,
Is turned into a big mess.

Whose kisses
Do you remember
That make
Your mouth water?
Why do you smile
Even when you're alone?
Tell me,
Who do you flirt with?
Tell me,
Who do you provoke?

Why so much distrust?
Perhaps it's a habit,
Perhaps it's the memories
Of all I've lived through
That bring me joy,
But I assure you,
There is no other reason.

You don't want my company
Where you go
If I only want
To protect and help you,
Who is waiting
And does for you
What I cannot?

Don't get me wrong,
But I like to do things
On my own.
I don't want to become
Dependent
And be a burden on anyone
If later patience is lost,
I am criticized
And it's thrown in my face.

You want a good lover,
And you want
Nothing to do with me,
You never make me feel
That I satisfy you,
Not even in deed.
Not even your words
Bring comfort
Or lead me to hope
Things will improve.
Of course,
You don't care what I do,
What I feel or how I live.

If you are good
Or bad lover,
I've never complained,
That,
Doesn't bother me.
I'd rather have
A good relationship
And well-founded
To a few minutes of pleasure
Well-marked by the clock.

I am going crazy,
I am obsessing,
And I cannot be.
I want everything
And have nothing with you.
What do you want with me?
What do you expect
From me?
If what you asked,
Was already given.

I want everything with you,
But we need
To know each other
As friends first.
Don't be blind
And don't be silly,
Neither do you ask,
Nor do I demand,
What we don't feel
Or give willingly.

I show you I love you
In a thousand ways
And you give
Only the crumbs.
You don't bother to know
What goes on with me,
You're so quiet with me,
Always indisposed.
Is it that the other one
Is as dumb as I am,
That he waits for his turn
At your disposition?

Your insecurity
Makes you say nonsense,
But I tell you I don't lie
And I don't hide anything,
So please,
Don't keep trampling
On my pride
With your harmful
And false accusations.
I don't want to regret
This relationship or the reason
We are together.

You deny me your kisses
When I need them most,
At times you ignore me
When I talk to you,
I don't get your attention
At the precise moment,
I don't get a caress
If I don't ask for it.
I am not a stick,
I am not of water,
I have a heart and soul
Like the one
Who keeps you away from me.
Tell me,
Who do you think of?
Who else seduces you?

At your age,
Your jealousy is ridiculous.
You are selfish and greedy,
You want everything
For you
And want me at your feet
One hundred percent
And don't even see
That my time
And affection
Are always divided
Among the house, work,
You and the children.

Such a big mistake
Was getting involved with you.
I wanted to make
A second intent
At forming a home,

But we carry
With the mentality
And problems
From previous
Relationships.
We watch the eyes,
The words and the omitted
For fear of the betrayal
Or loneliness
And the little affection
That could've been
Starts to dry up quickly.
Your unfounded jealousy
Is your mistake
And part of your character
That pushes me away
From you.
We cannot continue
As such,
With the distrust
And reproaches,
My conscience is clear
But obviously, yours is not.

December 11, 1996

The Eyes of Love

The eyes of love
See everything perfect.
I see you
As my ideal man,
And for you I am
The perfection
Made into a woman.

I am
Your longed dream,
And you are everything
I've ever wished for.
I don't need
Anything more
And you have won it all.

The ears of love
Don't hear evil,
Don't hear criticism,
The ears of love
Only hear
The echo of passion
In beautiful whispers
That is revealed
In actions and flattery.

The words of love
Don't hurt, don't harm,
The words of love
Are kind, are patient
And merciful.
The words of love

Make you dream,
Love, and yearn.
In the memories
That are left,
The words of love
Give us encouragement.

The heart of love
Doesn't give charity,
Doesn't give handouts,
Doesn't ask or demand
For what will come
Oh so patiently.

The angels of love
Touched us
With their wings
And gathered our souls,
You are the cause of my joy,
And I am the strength
Of your life.
You have everything
I've ever wanted,
And together
We start down a new path.
The eyes of love
See us as one on the road
Of your existence and mine.

October 1, 1996

Insecurity

Where there is love,
There is respect
For obligations,
Ideas, and rights.

Where there is love,
There is trust
To do and decide
For oneself
Without fear
To anything.

Where there is love,
There is kindness
That cares
And protects
Without injuring.

Where there is love,
There is liberty
To think, decide,
Say, and opt out
Without fearing
The reaction
Or what will be said.

Where there is love,
There is peace
In the conscience
And the home
And there is responsibility
In each resident.

Where there is love
For oneself,
There is happiness
That is felt by
And is transmitted
To others.

Where there is love,
There is God
And He's the force
That maintains
And makes changes.

Where there love
To God,
Nothing is missing
Because there is faith,
Truth, and hope.
There is spiritual peace,
Tolerance, patience,
Compassion,
And understanding.

Where
There are doubts,
Jealousy and control,
It's because the accuser
Has been around
But oppresses
With slandering
To cover its tracks
And to be the winner.

November 10, 1995

Silly Men

Men, men,
Silly men,
They search
For what they want,
They want
What they search,
But once they have it,
They complain, threaten,
Accuse and blame.

Men, poor men,
Selfish and cynical,
Want everything
On command
But give or return very little.
If things are not ready,
They abuse
Their physical power.

Silly men,
They make their rounds
But demand innocence,
So they talk afterwards
Of their experiences
And what they dislike.

Men, men,
Talk and criticize the facts,
Talk from their pain
When feeling the disdain
And their minimal wishes
Were abstained.

Men
Of little dignity,
Exaggerate and lie,
Publish and talk
Of the lovers they've had.
They feel victims
Of evil,
But are at the vanguard
And ready to attack.

Men
Of little value,
Pride and decency,
To look good
As vanquishers,
They wrong the women
Who see them bare naked.
Women end up as libertines
And men,
As the great masters.

Man, yes, you.
Only words are left
To feel superior
To the one who gave you
Affection, love
And companionship.
You talk out of anger
And pain,
And vengeance
Is in the tone of voice
As you see
In your loneliness,
Not even God is there.

Man, yes, you,
Understand
That praising yourself
By demeaning women
Are the worst kind.
Your honor
Is also destroyed
With each word
You divulge.
Better to be quiet and accept
What you construct.

February 9, 1997

Beauty And The Beast

No doubt,
The years of loneliness
Affected me
More than it seemed.
I became a mother
Devoted to my child
And with the routine of the home,
I became a recluse
Trying to prevent
Harsh criticism.

But in my silence
And within me,
I desired the attention,
Words, and flattery,
And the touch of a man
Who'd see in me
What I was.
I felt the loneliness
In my mind
But in my hands
I was hiding
The burning passion.

I didn't ask for much,
I only wanted to chat,
Maybe he'd touch my hand
And to the maximum,
Maybe get a kiss.
I asked for all this
Without saying anything
But I felt people

Could read my mind
And in my imagination,
I saw my faceless victim,
I saw the moments
In different scenes,
But I didn't see
Any suitors coming near.

Then, a man comes close
With the face of innocence,
A victim or hypocrite,
He wants a relationship,
Promotes his good traits
And gives the good points
Of his life,
I smiled to meditate
On what he offers.

THE SEDUCTION

His insistence and flirtation
Made me respond to him,
His compliments
Made me smile
And his touch
Seemed to burn my skin
Like embers of fire.

Kisses in the air
And the, *I love you so much…*
Came from his lips.
I responded
But not in the way he wished.
He said to see my beauty
And in his story
We were beauty and the beast

And we laugh freely
From nothing at all
As the images and words
Were great.

THE ENTRAPMENT

Between grievances
And more grievances,
He vents his sadness
And burdens,
His stories of a selfless man
And victim
From the infidelities
Of the women
He had loved before
Were never ending.

Now, he's penniless,
Homeless and no family,
And I accepted him.
Poor man,
He had nowhere to go,
All the bad happened to him
Like a season of failures
That don't end.

Patiently, I comforted
And encouraged him like a kid
And amid his complaints,
He heightened
His personal grandeur
But in his venting,
He started making plans
Of a future together
That suited the both of us.

THE CONTROL

This tale became a tragedy
Constant in drama.
The laugh just ended
And became sorrows,
Anger and anguish
When his jealousy
Wanted to control
My body, my thoughts,
My behavior and my time.

Phone calls at dawn,
Day or night,
Unexpected visits,
Unwanted help,
Suffocating protection,
Constant persecution,
Continuous surveillance,
Question and examination
Of my smiles,
What I said or kept quiet
And unexpected trips
To end up alone
Accused of deception
And I was reprimanded
For my silence
That he felt mysterious.

His evil came mixed
With self-victimization,
Wanting to be inside my head
To see what I thought,
Wanting me at his feet
And attached to him
So I wouldn't escape.

I owed myself respect
And I wanted to end
The relationship
Several times
But the exaggerated pain
On his face was pitiful.
'Give me a chance,
I'm going to change.
I love you so much
That I'm even jealous
Of the shadow
Accompanying you.'
He'd say in a broken voice
But the insecurity and control
Were revealing and prevailed.

Amid his perversity
Flattery came out,
But he demanded love,
Company, attention
And words of affection.
He wanted all of me
But gave nothing more
Than troubles.
'Tell me you love me,
Even as a favor.'
My silence
And my crossed hands
Were manipulated
To follow his game,
My hand over his heart
Or his head
And his face of pain
Made me see him
With suspicion and disgust.

He put the responsibility
Away from him and over me.
'It's that you're
Finger feeding me.'
He said with raw pain
In his face.
My ignorance
Made me ask him,
'What's that?'
And with a beggar's face
He responds,
'It means you give me
The crumbs of love
Little by little.'
But, how I could do
What I didn't feel like doing?

THE THREATS

His complaints, control
And manipulation
Wore me down
And patience was over.
I became strong
Like never before,
And I responded to him
In the same manner,
With that annoyance
And dry words
That a villain deserves.
Threats out of nothing,
With tone and posture,
Were well calculated.
'If you don't do
What I tell you,
Everyone will know

What you do with me.'
He learned
How to hurt me
And his repeated threats
Put my reputation at risk.

Words were incendiary
And threats didn't cease,
Emotional blackmail,
That's what it was.
'Leave me little by little
So it doesn't hurt as much.'
And I wanted to slam
The door shut
And undo the terror.

VENGEANCE

He wasted no time,
The scoundrel
Ran with the story
Of a suffering man
But, vengefully,
Dragged my name
Through the mud.
For those who listened,
I was the libertine
And he was a man of respect
And, because of this,
There were many wars,
New enemies
And people who thought
They were better than me,
And that's because I don't say
What I think of them.

ANALYSIS

He was correct,
He was a beast,
Ugly like his conscience
And brutally harmful
To my mind and spirit.
I was the perfect prey
For his aggression.
I was not conscious
Of the harm coming to me,
He took advantage
Of all he saw,
My body perspired
Loneliness,
My face showed
The lack of attention,
And my mind
Revealed me unshielded.

From being a good man,
He switched
To a provoked animal,
That became enraged
And his whispering screams
And blows
With a quiet hand,
Hurt and buried the affection
He never won.

I was saved
From a dreadful life,
Watching my everything
So that the master
Could live content.
But the master is not a man,

If, like a rogue,
He steals, probes,
Demands and orders
Then complains
And howls
Like a wolf in the jungle
When his demands
Are not met.

I learned the lesson well
And no man
Makes a fool of me again.
I opened my eyes
And got rid of that load
Hurting my back,
My legs and my soul.
It took time,
Effort and analysis
On the many incidents
To understand
That my self-esteem
Is a magnet
For the sexist man
And that, I have to change.

What I didn't say before,
I say it now,
The man
Who's free from sin,
May stand up
To make him holy
And make him an altar
Because the man
Who controls, betrays,
Lies and divulges,
Is wretched and coward.

Although I defend myself
With teeth and nails,
I see that unfortunately,
Some people don't see
That anger and jealousy
Deafen and blind
And kill the affection.
And, for love
To be good
And long lasting,
Should be given at will
And not by force
As love is won
With good deeds
And decency.

November 29, 1999

Blackout

Summer comes
With an incinerating heat
That's continually
Causing blackouts
When the heat is strongest.
In the middle of the afternoon,
The humidity and heat
Makes it like an oven
Outside of the home.

Night is falling
And the dark street
It looks calm.
The beau arrives
And shows concern
And, as a committed man,
He stays to take care of me.
He does not understand
That I don't need an escort
If by closing the door
Is enough.

Sitting on the threshold,
We talk
To get to know each other
And with time,
The talk and observations
On the neighborhood
Becomes repetitive.
Finally,
The beau leaves
By midnight

Feeling good and useful
Of having taken care of me,
Although he wasn't asked,
But he insists
That he is there
To help and protect me.

October 25, 1996

DAYDREAMS

A different future
Is wished
Amid
The daily problems
And quarrels
That cause unrest,
Amid
Frequent dilemmas
That seem heavy,
Amid
Complaints, reprimands,
Bickering, threats
And difficulties
That seem to never end.
Enigmatic images
And voices emerge,
Warm lighting is perceived,
Ghosts arise
That talk and answer me,
And daydreams arise
To take my mind
To another world
And other times
In an uncertain future.

Internet

In its beginnings,
When there was
Not much corruption
And social evil,
The internet arrived
As a fun tool.
It was connected
At my place
And it brought me friends
Suitors, opportunities
And knowledge.

In a troubled life,
Full of dramas,
Enemies and plots,
The internet was an escape
To the world
And an escape
From my world.
It made me daydream,
It was an attractive vision,
It was a thrill to touch,
And it was a breath
Of fresh air.

Soon, I was trapped
In an illusion,
And the internet
Was my guide
And my destruction.
I heard a caring voice
Coming out from a device

Say to me,
'Come, follow me,'
And I was coaxed
To followed him.
Unconsciously,
I fell in love with a shadow,
— A blurred image
Of someone unknown
But I loved the idea.

He spoke nicely
As needed,
I walked blindly
And I staggered
Because of him.
After a few words
And endless night of fun,
It all ended in a second.
Tragically,
It all disappeared
When I woke up,
The pain
In the ankle was real
But the pain
For that individual
Was imagined.

What tragedy it was,
I thought it was real
I wanted to touch him
And make him mine
But it was an illusion,
A dream, a fantasy.

December 31, 1998

Like An Angel

With the hands of an angel
You relieve my stress and pain,
With the ears of an angel
You quietly listen
To all my complaints,
With the words of an angel
You encourage and advise me
In every step I may take.

Like an angel friend
In my thoughts,
You make me feel
Positive about myself,
I trust you with the true me
Asleep or awake.

Like a guardian angel,
You're patient, kind and attentive,
Because of you I have faith,
Dreams, wishes and hopes.
You provoke the best of me
And because of you
I know angels
Don't offer or promise.
They just give.
That's you — with me

July 27, 1997

Today

At last,
The day has arrived,
You've given me your love
And today
Our souls come together
With modesty and love.

I give you
My sentiments pure,
Knowing you loving me
The same way.
There will be good times
And hard times,
But together
We'll defeat any adversity.

Today it all begins.
Solitude is behind us
And I thank the heavens
That I found the friend,
The lover, the mate,
Who fills with affection
My days.

January 28, 1995

United

With our souls pure
And flowers
In your hands,
In the altar
Of God and the people,
We promise love
Like in the past
And always.

The kiss
We share today,
Is proof of the love
That we show
With pride and honor.
Don't fear,
It's approved by God
And the guests.

The song of love
Is now playing.
Give me your hand,
My love,
And let yourself go
With the music
Of our memories
And end the night
In love the same.

Let the rounds
Of champagne
Never stop.
Let's toast,
If tomorrow
Brings adversity,
I know that united
We can defeat it.

I invite you to dream
And fulfill
Our future life.
United, beginning today,
As friends and lovers
If love is sincere,
Little is eternity.

Let's disappear
From the party
And take a trip
To the moon.
God willing,
On my behalf,
This union
Will have no end.
Your eternal lover
Assures you.

February 19, 1995

Again

Despite
My many years
And the bitter experiences
Of my life,
I am still trusting,
Still naïve,
Still like a child.

Although I have
Good teachers
And the lessons
Are interesting,
I still cannot pass the test.
Again, I fall
With the same kind of rock
And God,
From the heavens
Sees me and says,
'Oh, woman,
There you go again!'

I fell in love
With a ghost,
I fell in love
With a vision,
I fell in love
With an image,
With an illusion.
How stupid of me!
I cry for a love I don't know
And he doesn't see me
Or feel me.

With his words
Of affection,
I fell in the trap of love.
I feel my heart
Being pressed,
And I don't know
What's happening.
Where is my sanity?

How crazy!
An illusion
Makes me smile.
How awkward!
Another unforeseen deception.

August 15, 1997

With A Rose

With a rose in my hand
And trembling voice,
I am here to tell you
Of my feelings for you.

I meant to tell you
Before,
But I've been cautious.
Now I know,
This is the right time
And place
To tell you I really care.

It makes me happy
To have you near,
I feel sad when you leave.

Here, I am proposing
We get to know
Each other better
Because I'd like
To see you more often
In a personal manner.

March 20, 1997

And You Arrive

Submerged
In the frustration
And sadness of my life,
I had lost hope
Of loving
And being loved,
I isolated myself
From the world
And lived excluded
In my solitude
And deeply,
I accepted maturity.

And suddenly, you arrive.
With the love
Of a friend,
You made me feel assured
That the world
Doesn't forget
The nice words
That express tenderness.
Because of your
Beautiful motives,
I now feel ready
To offer and accept
Affection
With no commitment
Given.

Your name; Swordsman,
Impressed me.
A dueler, a fighter,

Skilled with the sword
And love.
And so, I saw you—
Strong, conqueror,
Invincible,
Who struggles and suffers,
But sees nothing
As impossible.

And you arrived
Like my hero.
With your signs of affection,
You save me
From my routine life
And melodramas.
Your sweet words conquer me,
I like the newness
Coming from you.

And you arrive
To my fairy tale.
I am the princess
And you are my Prince
Who brings down the walls
And overcomes the barriers.

And you arrive
Like the warrior of love.
You are like him,
Indomitable, powerful
And insistent.
Thanks to you,
I feel my heart beating.
You're kind and patient,
And I like your defiant
Knowledge.

And you arrive
Like the angel
Hiding behind the moon
And like the angel
That comes out
With the sun.
So you fill
My empty time
And makes it all better.

And you arrive
To my dreams.
I fall asleep
Embracing my pillow,
And I dream
I have you in my bed.
I kiss you, caress you,
Like there is no tomorrow.

And, again,
You arrive.
As I wake up
With your image
In my mind,
A smile
Comes to my face.
I feel like a teenager
As I remember
Your words,
I began to dream,
And unwillingly
I dream again
With the idea of love.

I like everything
About you.
I like you giving me
Your love in pieces.
I like your insinuations
And intimate thoughts.
I like the idea
That I can satisfy
Your forbidden wishes.

I'd like to see you pleased,
Because you're unique,
Because you're special,
I know
There's no other
Like you.
For you I'll fight
And bring down space
And time
I'll defeat all the burdens
For you.
I promise.

September 10, 1997

Here I Am

Here I am,
Staring at the phone,
Impatiently waiting
To hear a ring.

I glance at the clock
And see the needle
That mark the seconds
Move so very slow.

Here I am,
With my hopes high
To hear your voice
On the other end of the line.

Here I am, planning
Our entire conversation
And wondering
How you will respond.
It's urgent that we speak,
It's urgent
To hear your voice,
I can't hide my words
Of love anymore.

October 13, 1999

Honesty

I get nervous
Upon hearing your voice,
And I don't know
What to answer,
I've told you about my love,
You may remember.

I don't know you,
But I care for you.
If you said you'd come,
I'd be very happy, indeed.

I picture myself
As your lover
And your girlfriend,
I know I can make you happy,
If you'd let me.

Even if you have
Whom to think about,
You cannot stop me
From dreaming about you.
I miss you; I want you,
I tell you
But you are there, I am here,
You, taking pleasure in her
And I, pleading for you.

April 15, 1998

Passion
Is an emotional force
That incites and blinds
From what is needed,
From what is desired,
And we look for someone
To give our all
To feel peace
And satisfaction.
But passion,
Like any fling,
Is not long lasting or real.
Nonetheless,
Passion
Leaves very personal
Feelings
And unique pain.

November 2, 1998

Rain Of Love

The rain of love
Coming in sprinkles,
Like friendship and passion,
Brings joy and dreams
And makes romance resonate.
And the rain of love
Comes upon us
And falls on us
Swift, hard and heavy
And it remained
Until the clouds were emptied.

We showered
With warm water
Coming from up above
As the rain of love
And it purified our hearts.
The water ran slow
And made its way
From my body to yours
Forming runnels
And the tempest comes
That surrounds us
By black clouds
Ready to release its water.
The rain was for us
And us alone,
It followed our hands
And the steps we took.

The rain of love
Converts two quiet streams
Into one unrestrained river
And then,
They join their way
On route to the sea.
The sea unleashes its fury
And brings in more rain
And tempests
And it becomes a cycle
Of what life is
Like what friendship,
Love and passion is.

January 27, 1995

Cravings

I crave love,
I crave having company,
I crave
Many forbidden things,
I want a lover,
Wild, tender,
Passionate and wise
Of all my wishes.

I want a lover
Who'll make love
To my face, to my lips,
To my hands and to my body,
Who'll love me with a look,
With a smile,
With a touch full of fire.
I want to be seduced
With romance
And assaulted
With real passion.

I yearn for a lover
Whose kisses
Make me sigh.
I crave patient,
Soft and fragile kisses
I crave hungry kisses
Full of fire,
Strength and power
That leave me breathless.
I want him to steal a kiss
At any time and in any place.

I search for a lover
Who'll satisfy me,
I want everything
Emotionally,
I desire all in an instant
Inside my room
To not have the desire
To go in search
For stranger's things,
Just like me,
His unsatisfying heart
Will be filled with love.

I strive for a lover
Who'll conquer me each day
With simple things,
I need to be loved
Inside and out.
I want a lover
Who'll give me his all,
Not asking for a thing,
And all he does,
Does with no self-benefit
And even if he's had
Many experiences,
He'd show me his affection
With the purest innocence.

I need a lover
Who will see the world
Through my eyes,
A man who'll admire
My ideas and praise me
For what I do.
But to be honest
In his comments and answers.

I want a man
To be my hero,
Be my Prince Charming,
Who'll make me dream,
Who'll show me how to live,
And with him I see the light.
I would like a lover
Who, because of the love
He gives me,
Will feel proud and happy
To be whom he is.
I want someone
Who, with a word,
Can make me feel special
And who'd know
That for the world I am important,
And for him, I am essential.

I crave a sexual lover
Who'll love all of me,
A lover friend who'll listen
And be an adviser,
A lover mate
Who'll be helpful,
Understanding and honest.
I want a lover for always,
Who'll be brave and faithful.
I want a lover
Who, for what he may do,
Makes me dream.
I'll give all of me
To keep him happy and content.

July 16, 1995

This Heart

This heart
That complains much
And suffers,
Feels and cries,
Through letters,
The pain clears.

This heart
Is also grateful
And understands
The beautiful words
That incite smiles
In intervals,
And bring dreams
And hopes
For eternity.

November 10, 1999

Let Me

Let me take the venom
From your heart,
Let me rebuild
Your heart undone,
Let me be the muse
Of your inspiration.

Let me be the motive
For your passion,
Let me be the angel
Of your dreams,
Let me be the one
Who brings out
Your desires,
Let me be the friend
You would trust,
Let me be the one
With whom you laugh.

Let me change
Your disappointments
Into joys,
Let me be the toy
That you hug close,
Let me touch you
In dreams and reality,
Let me love you
For all eternity.

Let me free
All my hidden emotions,
Let me feel
The sensations
That I had written,
Let me paint my future
With the brush of your love,
Let me erase the turmoil
That time left behind.

Let yourself go
By the instinct
Of seduction,
Let yourself be guided
By care and love,
Let yourself be wanted
Today and always,
Let yourself be loved
With no barriers
And with no objections,
Let me win you over,
Let your imagination run,
And let me make you happy.

April 22, 1997

Virtues

Virtue is a quality,
It entails honesty
With oneself and others,
It is to appreciate and share
What we know and have,
Virtue is to respect
Other peoples' rights.

Virtue is personal,
It's improvement,
It's respect, decency
And discretion,
It's patience and mercy,
In one's attitude for others,
It's self-control
When speaking and reacting.

Virtue is prudence,
It's justice, strength
And temperance.
Virtue is love,
Faith, hope, and charity,
It's helping
Before help is needed,
When time indicates,
It's doing a good deed
For those who may need it.

Virtue
Is to recognize
Your mistakes
And admit to them
To whom will listen.
Virtue is to acknowledge
Those who deserve it.

Virtue is thankfulness,
It is to say from your heart,
I love you,
I am sorry,
I forgive you
Or *Thank you,*
And then leave aside
Any and all
Emotional garbage.

Virtue is to forgive
The offenses
It is to forget those words
That maintains
The pain tied up.
Virtue is to let go
Of the pain and rancor
And live in harmony.

Sexual virtue
Is innocence and virginity
Of the body and mind,
It is to surrender blindly
To the loved one
In a timely manner
And be loyal.

Virtue
Is to have few partners
But to love intensely,
It is to keep the mate happy
And do everything possible
To make the relationship work.

Virginity is not a virtue.
Perhaps no one
Has suggested
The forbidden,
Perhaps they haven't loved
Anyone enough
For intimacy,
Because when
We truly love,
We forget preconceptions,
Advice and criteria.

January 9, 1999

HALLUCINATIONS

The past
We have lived
Is a certain memory,
A set of nightmares,
Hallucinations
Or dead dreams.
The past
May leave proof
It existed
Leaving open wounds
That hurt forever.
The past
May be blocked
To prevent more pain
Or may be analyzed
To see our mistakes
And the process of things.

Charlatan

A poor fool
Fell in love with a man
Who turned out to be a charlatan
And she, dumb, innocent,
Ignorant and credulous,
Young and inexperienced
In social relationships,
Didn't see the symptoms
Or the consequences.

Her interest was firm
And revealing
But he fluctuated.
She didn't see the effect
In the months of chasing him
But he was kind of flirty,
Kind of distant,
Kind of talkative,
Kind of curt,
Kind of attractive,
Kind of unpleasant,
Kind of friendly,
Kind of anti-social,
Kind of interesting,
And kind of helpful.
At times he looked for her
And other times,
He kept away.

She did everything
To get his attention
But nothing seemed to work

To make him decide,
Nothing seemed to shift
The scale to her benefit
And his front
Was unwavering.
But a charlatan yields a bit
Seeing that the plaything,
He controls from afar,
Is about to make a turn
On the last steps of the race.

The charlatan
Takes the reins again
Of a relationship
That didn't seem to be
And with flattery
And words of love,
He makes the poor fool
Believe he's in love.
He sprinkles the conversations
And times
With kisses and the *I love you.*
The charlatan is manipulated
From above
And, like a puppet,
He does and moves as ordered.
The good about being in love,
Turns into a bomb of rage,
Always suspicious,
In any setting and time.
With the ear up and fed
By the unfounded accusations
And, with the mind filled,
He finds a good excuse
To cement his post,
His power and his title

While he confounds
His self-doubt
With a lover's jealousy.

Hypocrite like no other,
The charlatan, in public,
Was respectful
And was her right hand.
He was good company
That made her feel protected
And sure of herself
But in private,
He was a raging bull
And the demon
Of the nightmares,
Who made her feel the worst
With his screams
And many offenses.

The poor fool
Cries and gets angry
And always is to blame
But the charlatan's
Superficial apologies
Filled the air.
The high self-esteem
That the poor fool once had,
Now ran on the grounds
Like water
On burning sand.

Charlatan, yes he was,
He spoke of marriage
And children,
He filled her head
With dreams

And made her see his visions
But in the break-up,
It came out that he
Never loved her
And only pity kept him there.
He no longer wanted
His part of the problem
As he had other goals
And, by his choice,
Never took responsibility
For what should've been.
The man was a charlatan,
Coward, facetious
And conniving,
Who said to love
The poor fool,
Now says all this
Was manufactured stories
And chose to be her enemy
At the moment of the break up.

Pitiful charlatan,
A vile man
Makes excuses and stories,
Pretends, invents and lies
To look good
And not have a guilty
Conscience.
It's evident,
For him not to be alone
And see his failed life,
He mates, uses and discards
Those who love him
And are near.
He will deny his true being
As, who would stay

In a relationship for pity
But shows love,
Unity and jealousy?

A charlatan
Lies, lies, lies,
Deceives and cajoles,
For a charlatan,
Sneaky and traitor,
The break-up
And the farewells
Are quick and easy
When there's a substitute.
However, even if he wants
To live a decent life,
To not be alone,
A charlatan
Will do anything
And please anyone
Because he's afraid of the dark.
He never knows what he had
And what he destroyed
Making himself the victim
But watching out
That it's not done to him
What he did to others.

November 27, 1998

Negligent

Negligent man,
Set me aside for a later time,
Possessive mate,
Set me in my place
When he said,
I got out of hand,
Negligent lover,
Didn't realize what he had
Until it was too late.

Negligent man,
Undecided for everything,
Procrastinate on every issue
Putting for later what might be.
Negligent man
Became negligent father
To please the woman
That is stronger than him.

September 18, 1993

Realization

I felt a winner
For having him,
I felt successful
Because he chose me
Among all his admirers.
I felt happy
Because the man I love,
Now loves me.

I was willfully
Blind and dumb,
I yielded, I surrendered
To his command
As the words of love
Entered my mind,
I always overvalued
The caresses and the acts,
I let myself be defeated
By the *I love you*
That he professed
And I didn't see
The ill intentions
Or hypocrite outcomes.

I felt complete
For having him
In my life and by me,
I thought I was happy
And he brought me happiness
But I didn't see
The minutes of laughter
And good temperament

Were shaded
By screams, dictatorship
And his finger on my face
Blaming me of everything.

I thought he
Gave me security
And raised my self-esteem
But I didn't see
That, among his compliments,
Came the criticism,
Complaints, insults and threats.
I didn't see
That I lived vigilant
To not cause anger
Or incite any fights.

I thought
The jealousy scenes
Were from love,
I didn't see his jealousy
Was a way of control,
I didn't see
It was from his low self-esteem.
I thought his control
Was love and protection,
I didn't see it was a cover
To keep me at bay.
I thought his anger
Had a reason,
I didn't see how weak
And coward he really was
As he fought with me
And showed off his strength.

I thought he brought
The excitement and fun
To my monotonous life
And I took affection
To what I was learning from him.
I thought I didn't need
Other people
Because he offered
What seemed long lasting.
I didn't see the wickedness
Of isolation,
I didn't see the manipulation
In his behavior.

I thought he'd be
The keeper of my secrets,
Fears, weaknesses,
Dislikes and whims
But I didn't see
And didn't understand
That he was the word spreader
Of what I did and said.

I thought he gave me
The place I deserved,
I thought he gave me direction
And I'd be lost without him
In the crowds or in my daily life,
I didn't see
That he halted my steps.

I thought he gave me
The physical
And mental strength
To do, to speak
And to defend myself.

I thought he made me strong
For the affection
He gave me
And the attention
He paid to me,
I thought he kept me safe.
I didn't see
That affection was pricey,
And his attention
Gave me no respect
And I was not safe.

With time
I came to the realization
That the strength,
Happiness, security
And integrity,
I have it all,
And it comes from within.

December 28, 1999

Wars

The man who smiled
So flirtatiously,
Filled me with kisses,
Caresses and beautiful words,
Had me cajoled
With his words of love.
The man who said
To find reminders of me
In the songs he heard,
Was jealous of everyone
From loving me so much,
Didn't want to share me
With anyone
And demanded my honesty
To feel secure,
—That same man
Lied to me in every aspect,
He never meant what he said.

The man who had
My blind loyalty,
Had my time, my attention
And my love at his disposition.
The man who didn't understand
My point of view, my words
Or my eagerness to see him,
Frequently told me
I lived in LaLa land
For wanting affection,
—That same man
Now lies through his teeth.

The man who said
To love me and spoke
Of marriage and children,
Promised to never hurt me
When he said to want
To grow old with me.
The man who often said
I was his best friend
And couldn't live without me,
Was my lover and my friend,
—That same man
Slammed the door
And fled like a criminal
When he had another offer.

The man who pretends
Loyalty, sincerity and hurt,
Cried 'Poor me' to the family
Who covers up for him,
And denied to love me
To start a new life
With no recriminations.
The man who claimed
Victimhood to the woman
And to me,
Was the carrier of the gossip
And put us against each other.
The man and his people
Who accused me
Of moral and legal crimes
To appear innocent,
—That same man,
With their help,
Dragged my name and pride
Through the mud
With the slandering.

The man who never accepted
Orders from me,
Seemed brave, secure
Strong and independent
When flaunting his sexism
Against my weakness.
The man who taught me
To depend on him
Thus later he'd throw in my face
All the favors done,
In his low points,
Cried for me not to leave him
But could not get rid of her,
The man who's now
Obedient to her
And doesn't think,
Doesn't go and doesn't do
Anything alone,
Comes as part of the package,
Now lives by the rules,
Desires and whims
Of a naff woman,
—That same man
Is now my public enemy
Number one
And the woman is number two.

The man who asked me
For another chance
And said he wanted to be
A father to our child,
Forgot that time is golden
And words are a burden
That count dearly.
The man who was forbidden
To show up for the birth,

Later made-up excuses
To not see his first-born child
Would not dare disturb the peace
With a controlling woman,
—That same man
Met his child
On the side of the road.

The man who set
The child aside
And said he'd see
What he could do for the child
At a later time,
Kept quiet and distant
Even living close by.
The man who was uninterested
Or unaware in legal matters,
Threw fits of rage
For the child support
And demands full custody
As he wants revenge
In every possible way.
The man who's advised
By her past experiences,
Comes backed by family
To appear as a good son
And good father,
—That same man and her
Are monstrous liars
In the courtroom.

The man who never paid
Attention to my writing,
Now dissects my every word
To contradict them with lies,
And twists my words to his favor,

And alter memories and facts.
The man who called the cops
At every exchange
For a risk and danger
That's only in his mind,
Involved me in made up crimes
And brings fake witnesses.
The man who had the judges
And the cops on his side,
Smiles nicely and peacefully.
In the courtroom,
He speaks with a soft voice,
Freely and at length,
And was winning the case
Based on lies and exaggerations,
—The same man
Turned out to be a good actor
As he gives me a devilish smile
And laughs at me
But in the courtroom
He's like an angel.

The man who fought,
To keep the child
Was never present
To enjoy or watch him
But was impatient and angry
With the child
Because when things are done
Out of vengeance,
There is no space or motive
For understanding.
The man who thought
I was incompetent and weak,
Thought I would give up
And relinquish my child so easily

But he was wrong,
He doesn't see that as a mother,
I am invincible,
—That same man
Really got to know me
When I gave the last blow.

Shame I didn't see it
As it was happening
Because it seems I have lived
A life of wars
Fighting the family
To love the man.
I lived fighting the man
For his stupid sexism
That leaves nothing but sorrows.
I lived fighting the man
To love my child
As the father he is
But I couldn't prevent my child
From rejection and negligence.
I lived fighting the system
That doesn't want to see the evil
And the consequences
Of an emotional vengeance
As a man who wants to be
A father to the child,
Gives him time, respect,
Security and love
From the beginning
And never sets him aside
Or for a later time.

December 31, 1999

Suffocation

I've cried much
Because of the past
And now, such is the anger
That I live with a sour taste
In my mouth.
The past is like an entity
That doesn't leave
And won't leave me alone,
It's ruthless and vindictive,
It fights and argues
For stupidities
But the only one affected
Is my son.

The wars with the past
Don't decrease
And don't end,
They're continuous
And consistent
And just looking at him,
Upsets my stomach.

These legal wars,
All the hearings
And requirements,
The searching, the process
Of submitting paperwork,
Have been emotionally fatiguing,
Time consuming
And very expensive,
I've always been poor
But this, literally, ruined me.

I live suffocated
As if I lived in a dungeon
With the lights off,
It's a suffocation
As if I was in the desert
At 200 degrees,
I feel suffocated
As if I had received
A blow in my stomach
And the impact
Left me breathless.

I need
To pave my way
To breathe again,
I need to think of me
And my son,
I need to escape
And leave this bulk
Of problems behind,
I need to set foot on freedom
For my mental state.

July 2, 1999

124

Uncertainty

How sad it is
To hear the words,
'I don't love you,
I don't love you anymore,
I never loved you,
I am in love
With someone else,
From your own doing,
I will never come back.'
The world collapses,
The noises become muffled,
The vision gets blurred,
A cold air
Blows into my soul.
It makes me tremble,
And a freezing feeling
Travels from my head
To my toes.
A weight falls on me
That leaves me immobile,
A big knot on my throat
Doesn't let me speak,
And my veins get entangled,
The blood doesn't go
To my heart,
I am choking,
– I cannot breathe.

Should I cry or be angry?
Should I ask questions
Or remain silent?
The frequent flattery

To my smarts and beauty,
Was it really ever felt
Or was it to keep me
Under the spell?
How can the man
Tell me he doesn't love me
If he told me
He loved me every day?
Is he lying now
Or was he lying then?
Is he being forced
To be rude and indifferent
Or was he pressured
To tell me
He loved me then?

Were all those kisses
And embraces fake?
The complete surrendering
When making love,
Was that from a fraud
And an impostor?
The protection
And possessiveness,
Was it a way
To keep me enthralled
Or was he truly a caring man?
The insecurity
And the jealousy scenes,
Were they truly felt
Out of love
Or was that a performance
To protect his manliness?
Did he ever want me for him
Or was the loneliness
More intimidating?

The words
Love,
Best Friend,
Marriage,
Children
And *Forever,*
How can they be said
If were not meant?
The plans and dreams
Of forming a home
And family,
Were those a lie
Or is he forced to deny
What seemed to be true?
The words of marriage
And children,
How could they be
Repeatedly mentioned
If they were not wanted
Or ever felt?
Is he forced to lie now
Or was he compelled
To live a lie then?

Now he says
He doesn't love me,
Is he being honest
With himself,
Or is he doing exactly
What the new mate
Expects of him?
Is he being forced
To perform the roll
Of a cold-blooded man
Or are his words in revenge
As I undid the relationship?

But, the most important
Question is,
If he never loved me,
Why did he ask me
To be his girlfriend?
Why couldn't he just
Wave goodbye at me
From a distance
And let me be
For someone else?

May 3, 1991

Hurt

The hurt of loving someone
And being enchanted
By the sparkle in his smile,
The twinkle in his eye
And the lies he told,
Is overwhelming.

The hurt of letting the man
Lead me and push me
Into the abyss, is appalling
As I was sure he loved me
And he was the hero
Who'd save me
Before the tragedy.

The hurt of being yelled at,
Disrespected, diminished,
Underappreciated,
And scolded until I cried,
Is soul crushing.

The hurt of being secluded
To avoid the rage of jealousy,
Kills the mind
But a word of affection
Is the best thing to revive
And it's the best cover up
To make myself believe
I am loved.

The hurt of abruptly
Ending a relationship
And the hurt of being blamed,
Never goes away.
The pain is so vivid
Everything else is opaque,
It left me empty-handed,
Heart-broken
And self-reprimanded.

The hurt of being betrayed
And being lied to,
Never subsides,
But the hurt to know
He speaks ill of me
When he never said
Anything to my face,
Is excessively deep.

The hurt of trying
To understand him
And hearing his complaints
Unfavorable to her,
Is not satisfying or consoling.

The hurt of being asked
To rid myself of the package
To ease his problems
As he's been twice presented
With the same surprise,
Leaves me speechless,
Dazed and aghast.

The hurt of hearing his regrets
And make vague promises
Of him returning
And then, later having me
Waiting for him in vain

And not seeing
His disinterest in my pain,
It's emotional confusion.

The hurt of hearing
The crude words,
'I don't love you,
I've never loved you,'
Come out of the mouth
That used to kiss me,
Is insidious from his part
And makes an asphyxiating
Knot in my throat.

The hurt of attempting
To control my emotions
But feel the tears
Roll down unexpectedly,
Is ridiculously stupid,
Disgraceful and disappointing.

The hurt of giving birth
And seeing my baby
So tiny and defenseless
And feeling I am so alone,
Is overwhelming.

The hurt of knowing
My child needs the father
And his side of the family,
Is powerful
But the hurt of seeing
That I take my child to them
And they postpone all
For a later date,
It's a pain I cannot explain.

The hurt of going to court
For the custody of my child
Because they want revenge,
Is unbearable.

The hurt to see
The man does everything
To please a woman
Who has nothing
To do with this matter,
Is excruciating.

The hurt to see
The courts have no time
Or patience for me
And side with the man,
Unloving and negligent,
Is very deep.

The hurt to see
So much money wasted
Defending myself
And protecting my child
From an ungrateful man,
Has no end.

The hurt of seeing
I could lose my child
With lies easily told
From a smiling face,
Is frightening.

The hurt of understanding
That I've been
Begging people
For their affection, approval

And acknowledgement
And, in that action,
I've taken my child
To be a victim and witness
To their indifference,
Is a wrenching hurt.

The hurt of living
With regrets
Has left open wounds
That don't heal
And deep long scars,
Hidden and visual,
In my mind.

The hurt from realizing
I've spent many years
Crying for and because
Of a worthless man,
Is incisive and priceless.

The hurt of realizing
All the years, emotions
And dreams wasted
In a one-way relationship,
Is exaggeratedly immense
And has no words
To describe it.

The hurt to know
He, so carelessly,
Made a new life
And here I was,
Holding on to every memory
And clinging
To the faint image of him,

Is eye opening
To the self-destruction.

The hurt of analyzing
My life
And seeing
I've woken up
And realize
That he's no longer mine
Or he never was,
Is a burden off my soul
And, finally, I feel free.

So, Lord,
I pray every night
To make me strong and wise
To defeat the man
And his people
Who never appreciated
Anything.

March 7, 1998

Flames

The flame of love,
That kept us cozy,
Warm, energized and alive,
Burned out
A long time ago
And now,
Only the cinder flakes
Of hatred
Flow in the air
And settle with the dust.

The flame of hope
That kept us working,
Blew out
And, in the darkness,
Disappointment
Left a big burn
In my heart
And unwellness in my mind.
The beautiful world
That I used to see
Is now ugly and aggressive.

The flame of dreams
That kept me moving,
Extinguished
One summer day at dawn.
With the rude awakening,
I realized
I was alone and lonely,
Unprotected and uncared for.
And now,
I find myself

In the middle
Of the battlefield
Dodging
The arrows and bullets
With my shield.

August 20, 1996

Dead Love

Love may move away
Or leave, be killed or die,
Disappear, vanish
Or, simply, be put away
In the wardrobe
Like an old box
Full of memories.

When love is strong,
It's alive and burns
And something forbids
Discarding of it
Into the void
Or into oblivion.
Love doesn't really die,
It's kept in the mind
And in the soul
And, on top
Of those feelings,
We lay
Big and heavy objects
So love won't escape
And betray us.
But, from the love, bliss,
Pleasure and lust
We once felt,
We now have pain,
Resentment and questions.

When love is for vanity,
The truth is glaring
That love out of deception,

Has no future nor gives life.
The deceiver
Deceives himself,
Thinking he's powerful,
He forbids, demands,
And exploits
The sentiments of his prey
But watches very closely
So they don't do to him
What he's done to them.

When the lover is wicked,
Like a criminal
With no conscience,
He kills the love
Of the one who loved him
And divulges it
As his big accomplishment
And he comes out blameless.
When the relationship ends,
His eyes reflect
Anger, selfishness
And vengeance.

In the name
Of everything we lived through
And for sake of the sprout
Already seeded,
I asked to be civilized,
For sake
Of the circumstances,
I ask to make peace,
For sake of what we once had,
I ask to be polite
But words are twisted
And the answer

Comes rushed and direct.
With a diabolical smile,
The lover spits attacks,
Scoldings and threats
With no end.
He reminds me
I should've thought
Of this long before
And says we are enemies
And we are at war.

… And the love saved
Among many secrets,
Is taken out of the box
And brought outside
To see it in the light of day.
I shake it
To give it some air
And, in my hands,
In front of my eyes,
I see the petals, leaves,
Stem and roots
All dried up,
Becoming only weeds.

December 15, 1998

Ungrateful

Some people
Are happy to overpower
The submissive and weak
Until they cry,
Yet, those same people,
Are never grateful
That, despite of it all,
They are loved.

Some people
Are not grateful
For the children
They bring into this world,
Instead,
Those same people
Want to nip it in the bud
Before giving them
A chance to fly.

Some people
Meddle and intrude
In others' relationship
To cause problems
And destroy
What is in process
And those same people
Only see
What they don't like
But don't appreciate
That their kin
Is taken care of
And is loved.

Some people
Speak from the teeth out
And the promises
Of helping and supporting
The child to be born
Is soon forgotten.
Those same people
Have no conscience
Of the rush of time
And don't appreciate
The child was brought
And presented
At their doorstep.
Note is taken
That hypocrisy,
Negligence
And lack of fortitude
Start to be visible.

Some people
Want no responsibility
And have no time
To invest in a child
From the woman
They dislike.
Those same
Ungrateful people
Don't see
Their contribution
To the social dislike
And don't see the good
Of each person,
Defect or no defect.

Some people
Are ungrateful
And vindictive
And want to step over
The one they said to love.
Those same people,
Even if they show off
Their strength,
Are weak and dumb
On their own.
They want and need
To have a mate
Feeding their ego
Because they
Did not believe
The flattery or love
In the voices
From the past.

Some people,
When they're in trouble,
Look for the one
They rejected before.
They ask to join forces,
Knowledge, power
And resistance
Against the monster
They call kin.
Those same people,
When their case
Is resolved,
Selfish and ungratefully,
Turn their back
On the one
Who helped them
Claiming

Blood is thicker than water
And don't listen
To anything else.

Some people
Only have short memory
And when they see the
Son is in trouble
With the new mate,
They compare,
In every way,
The previous
And the current woman
And shamelessly ask
To take back the man
Who was fraudulent
And ungrateful
Just like them.
Entire clan
Of ungrateful people,
They are,
They didn't see
The good they had
In front of their eyes.

Some people
Don't realize
How ungrateful they are.
Their hypocrisy
And bias
Cover their eyes
To how low
They truly are.
Neither they see
The submissive and weak,
At some point,

Becomes strong
And defiant.
No doubt about it,
Some people
Are very ungrateful,
Despicable
And a disgrace in society.

October 17, 1998

Printed in the USA
CPSIA information can be obtained
at www.ICGtesting.com
LVHW090748270324
775599LV00001B/188